Arbeitsblätter für den berufsbezogenen Englischunterricht

Technisches Englisch 2

Hubertus Bleich

westermann

1. Key to the work sheets

Lesson			Page
Engines – from steam to CIM			**4**
2.5	Steam engines		4
2.6	Petrol engines		6
2.6	Diesel and jet engines		8
2.7	Electric motors		9
	Option 1:	A car cooling system	11
	Option 2:	How do gears work? – How do brakes work?	12
	Option 3:	Engines – World-field exercise	13
2.8	**Revision Unit:**	**Engines**	14
		Vocab-check	15
Computers			**16**
2.9	Basic Elements		16
2.10	New methods of production: CAD, CAM, CIM		18
	Boeing's computer aided design		21
	Explanation and language practise		22
	Option 1:	Fibre optic cables	23
	Option 2:	World-field exercise "computer memory"	25
2.11	**Revision Unit:**	**Computers**	26
		Vocab-check	27
Electricity			**28**
3.1	**Toolbox 1:**	**Electricity**	28
3.2	Electricity supply		30
	Option 1:	Electrical repairs	33
	Option 2:	How to install a socket	35
	Option 3:	How does a transformer work?	36
		How does an electromagnet work?	36
3.3	**Revision Unit:**	**Electricity**	37
		Vocab-check	39
Metalwork			**40**
3.4	**Toolbox 2:**	**Metalwork**	40
3.5	Methods of welding: Gas and arc welding		42
3.6	Methods of welding: Safety instructions		44
3.7	Soft and hard soldering		46
	Option 1:	How to put up a shelve	48
	Option 2:	How to drill a hole in a steel plate	49
3.8	**Revision Unit:**	**Welding and soldering**	50
		Vocab-check	52
Plumbing			**53**
3.9	**Toolbox 3:**	**Plumbing**	53
3.10	Plumbing – Everything spick-and-span		55
Building and plastering			**57**
3.11	**Toolbox 4:**	**Building and plastering**	57
3.12	What is cement made of? – How is concrete made?		59
	How to prepare a foundation for a brick wall		60
	How to mix concrete by hand		61
	Toolbox 5:	**Woodwork**	62
	Security around the house		64
	The British vocational system		68

Lesson 2. Vokabeltests

Lesson		Page
– Vorlage		74
– Engines	Test A und B	76
– Computers	Test A und B	78
– Electricity	Test A und B	80
– Welding and soldering	Test A und B	82

Lesson 3. Word Games

3.1. Crosswords	3.2. Search-a-word	Page
		84
– Engines	– Engines	84
– Computers	– Computers	85
– Electricity	– Electricity	86
– Welding and soldering	– Welding and soldering	87
– Lösungen		88

Lesson 4. Kopiervorlagen für OH-Folien

	Page
1. Thomas Newcomen	92
2. Slide valve	93
3. Four-stroke petrol engine	94
4. Electric motor	95
5. Computers – basic elements	96
6. Computerized design and production	97
7. Welding	98
8. The bathroom – spick-and-span	99
– Toolbox 1 – Electricity	100
– Toolbox 2 – Metalwork	101
– Toolbox 3 – Plumbing	102
– Toolbox 4 – Woodwork	103
– Toolbox 5 – Building and plastering	104

Lesson 5. Zusatztexte für Klassenarbeiten, Tests, Stillarbeit, Hausaufgaben ...

		Page
5.1. The history of steam power	(Engines)	105
5.2. Electric cars or hybrid engines?	(Engines)	106
5.3. Air-conditioning and industrialization	(Electricity)	107
5.4. Computer viruses	(Computers)	108

Lesson 6. Vokabular Englisch – Deutsch

109

Engines 1 – Steam engines – past

Lesson **2.5.1**

Hero
(Greek philosopher and scientist)

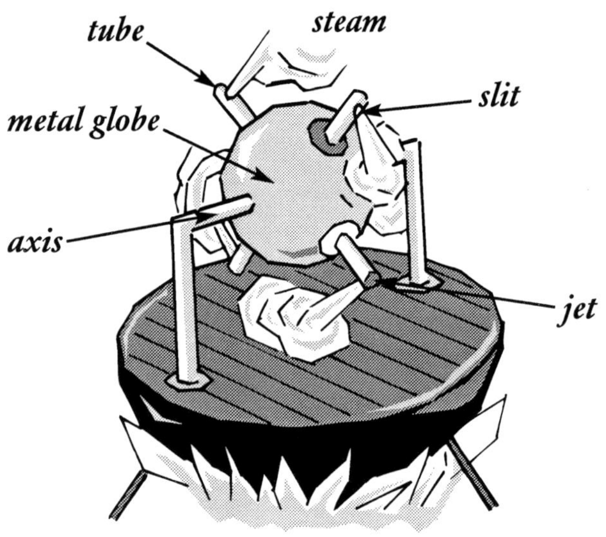

The machine *consists* of a hollow metal globe. The globe *can spin* around its metal axis. On the tubes there *are* several tubes with right angles to it. The end of the tubes *are* closed, but they *have* slits at the sides. The slits *work* as jets. Hero *fixes* the whole machine on a kettle full of water. A fire underneath *heats* the kettle. The steam *passes* through the axis into the globe and into the pipes. The steam *rushes* out of the jets and turns the globe around its axis. It *works*, in fact, the same way as a modem jet engine. In a jet engine hot gases *rush out* of the engine and thus *propel* it.

It is easy to understand how much Hero amazed his contemporaries with his magic machine. But he never used it **to drive** another machine. It was just a scientific toy.

Thomas Newcomen
(1663-1729)

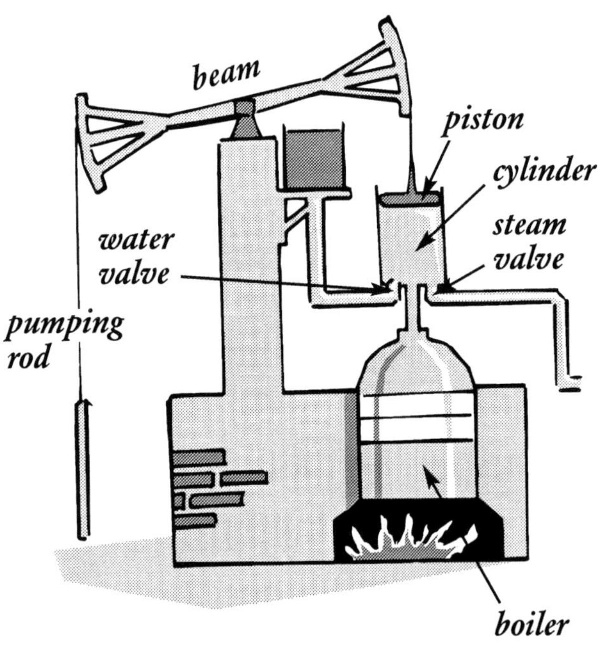

An English blacksmith invented the forerunner of the modern steam engine. He called it a fire engine. He used it to pump water from mines.

Newcomen´s engine *works* like a seesaw. He *fixes* a pumping rod to one end of a beam and the piston to the other end. The piston *is* in a cylinder with a steam valve at the bottom. Under the cylinder *is* a boiler. The weight of the pumping rod *pulls* the piston up. Steam *passes* through the open steam valve and *fills* the cylinder. Then a man *closes* the steam valve and *opens* the water valve for a moment. A tiny jet of cold water *rushes* into the cylinder and *condenses* the steam and this *makes* a partial vacuum inside the cylinder, so that the atmospheric pressure *presses* the piston down. Then a man *opens* the steam valve again and the piston *goes* up again. Thus the engine *causes* an up-and-down movement of the pumping rod.

It made 12 **strokes** a minute and could raise 50 gallons of water from a depth of 160 feet. Two men had **to operate** the machine: one had to attend to the fire and the other, usually a small boy, had to open and to close the valves.

1. *Copy the underlined technical terms. Label the drawings.*
   Then use these words to explain the function.
2. *The text uses past tense for the explanation for the systems. Rewrite the articles using present tense.* *(s. o.) (Passiv ebenso möglich)*
3. *What effect did the invention of steam power have on the future technological development after James Watt in 1769?* *Antwort unter Zusatztexte Nr.1 "The history of steam"*

Engines 1 – Steam engines – present Lesson 2.5.2

A steam engine ...*utilises*... the energy contained in steam under high pressure. The energy that is released when steam ...*expands*... is made to ...*produce*... rotary motion which can be used for the driving of machinery.

The steam from a boiler is ...*admitted*... into the cylinder in which there is a piston and in which the steam expands, causing the piston to move. When the piston has ...*travelled*... to the end of the cylinder and thus ...*completed*... its stroke, the now expanded steam is allowed to ...*escape*... from the cylinder. At the same time the steam is changed over, live steam under pressure being admitted to the other side of the piston, causing the piston to travel back until it has ...*reached*... the other end of its stroke. A steam engine of this kind is called "double-acting" because the force of the steam is applied alternately on both sides of the piston. While the piston is being forced in one direction by the expanding steam, the spent steam is ...*pushed*... out of the cylinder on the other side.

To make sure that the steam always is let in at the appropriate side of the cylinder a control device has been ...*installed*... : the flat slide valve.

1. Fill in the correct verb forms.
(es werden nicht alle benötigt)

to allow – *erlauben*
to be admitted – *eingelassen werd.*
to be driven – *angetrieben werden*
to be forced – *gedrückt werden*
to be installed – *angebracht sein*
to be pushed – *geschoben werden*
to cause – *verursachen*
to complete – *vervollständigen*
to contain – *beinhalten*
to escape – *flüchten*
to expand – *ausdehnen*
to produce – *erzeugen*
to reach – *erreichen*
to travel – *sich bewegen*
to utilise – *benutzen*

2. Then underline present passive forms.

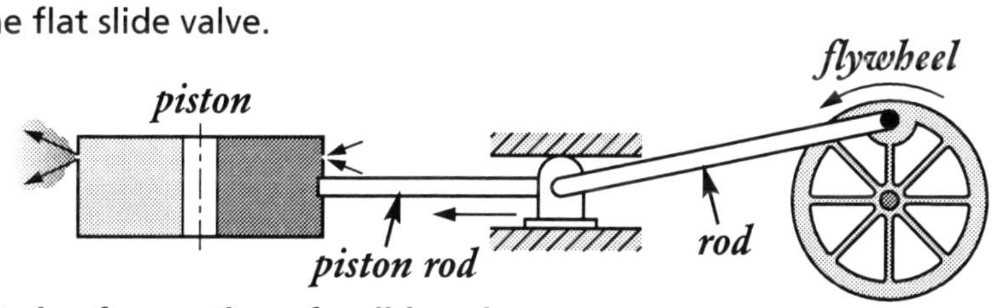

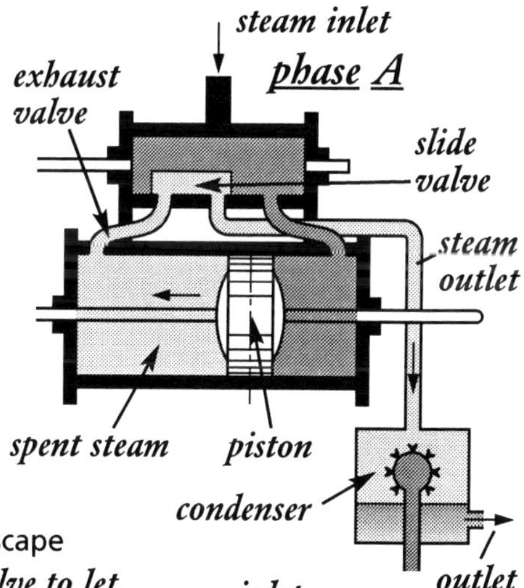

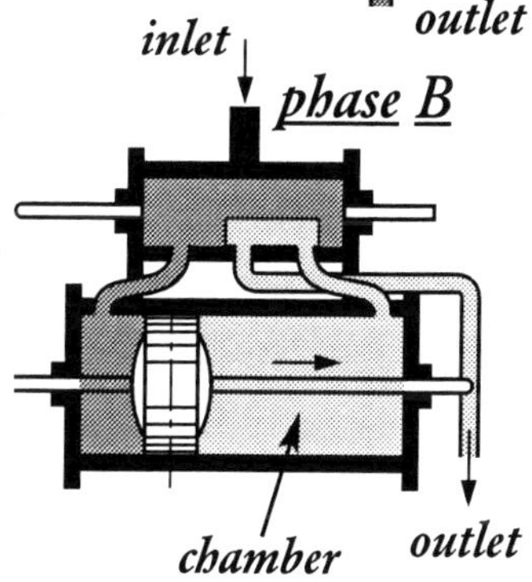

Mode of operation of a slide valve
(Form complete sentences.)

During / piston movement / to open / exhaust / spent steam / to escape
During the piston movement the slide valve opens the exhaust valve to let the spent steam escape.

At the same time / to open / one chamber / to let in / live steam
At the same time it opens one chamber to let live steam in.

It / alternatively / to cover / inlet port / exhaust port / to move / to and fro
It alternatively covers inlet and exhaust port and thus moves to and fro.

To be controlled / linkage / crankshaft / valve / to move / opposite / piston
It is controlled by a linkage from the crankshaft so that the valve moves in the opposite direction of the piston.

Spent steam / to pass / a condenser / to cool / water / to emerge
The spent steam is passed to a condenser where it cools down and later emerges as water.

Today steam engines are only used in cases where slow-running machinery with varying power requirements has to be driven, e.g. for winding gear in coal mines, ships propulsion machinery etc.. The efficiency in terms of utilisation of the contained energy is very low.

Engines 2 – Petrol engine

Lesson **2.6.1**

1. Identify the parts of this engine using the words from this list.

catalytic converter	Katalysator
combustion	Verbrennung
to compress	verdichten
camshaft	Nockenwelle
crankshaft	Kurbelwelle
cylinder	Zylinder
distributer	Zündverteiler
to escape	entweichen
exhaust valve	Auslassventil
flywheel	Schwungrad
to ignite	entzünden
to inject	einspritzen
inlet valve	Einlassventil
maintenance	Wartung
piston	Kolben
service	warten
spark	Funke
spark plug	Zündkerze
toxic	giftig

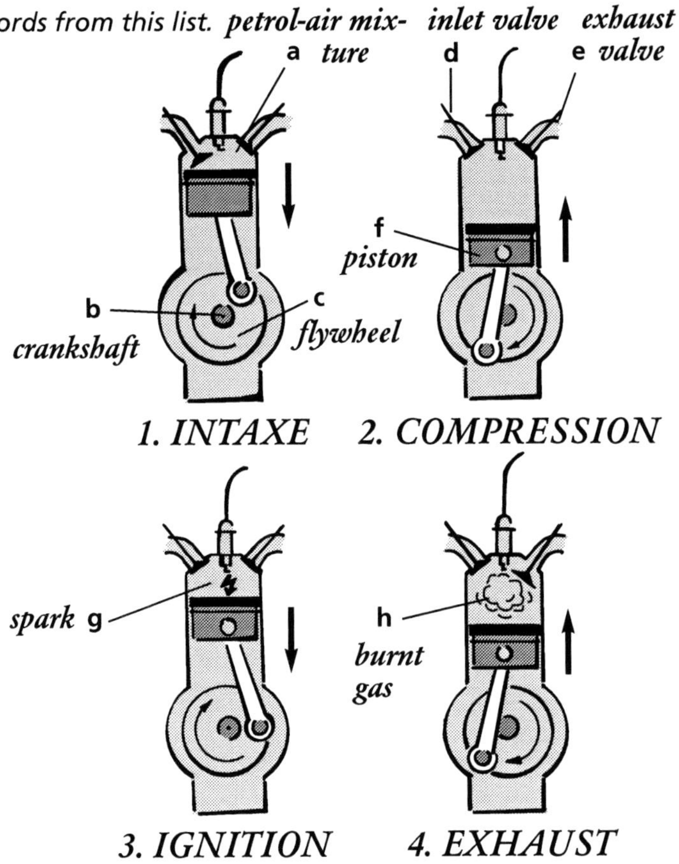

The engine works on four strokes. It burns a mixture of petrol and air which explodes in a cylinder. Inside the cylinder there is a piston which moves up and down. The engine is cooled by air or water.

The link is piston - crankshaft - camshaft - distributor - transmission system. The pistons drive the crankshaft, the crankshaft drives the camshaft and the camshaft drives the distributor.
The crankshaft is the link with the transmission system, which sends the power to the wheels.

2. Answer the following questions.

1. How does a car-engine work?

It burns a mixture of petrol and air which explodes.

2. What is inside the cylinder?

Inside the cylinder is a piston which moves up and down.

3. What do you know about the system?

The engine works on four strokes: Intake, compression, ignition and exhaust.

4. What's the link with the transmission system?

The link is the crankshaft which drives the camshaft.

Engines 2 – Petrol engine

Lesson **2.6.2**

3. Fill in the missing words.

The four *stroke* petrol engine burns a mixture of *petrol* and *gas* in a cylinder.

Inside the cylinder is a *piston* which moves up and down.

The engine is cooled by *air* or *water* .

These parts of an engine are electrical: *battery* , *spark plug* , *distributor* .

4. Everything correct? If not, please correct it.

1. Intake stroke. *(correct)*
The piston moves down and the mixture of petrol and air is pulled into the cylinder through a valve.

2. Compression stroke. *(wrong)*
The cam closes the inlet valve, the piston moves up and ~~depresses~~ *compresses* the mixture.

3. Power stroke. *(wrong)*
The spark plug ignites the mixture and it explodes. The piston is pushed ~~upwards~~ *downwards* and ~~holds~~ *turns* the crankshaft.

4. Exhaust stroke. *(wrong)*
The piston moves up ~~and down~~ and the burnt gases are pushed out of the cylinder through the open valve.

5. Look at the diagram of a four-stroke petrol engine one more time.

1. Identify the parts of the engine **remembering** the word list.

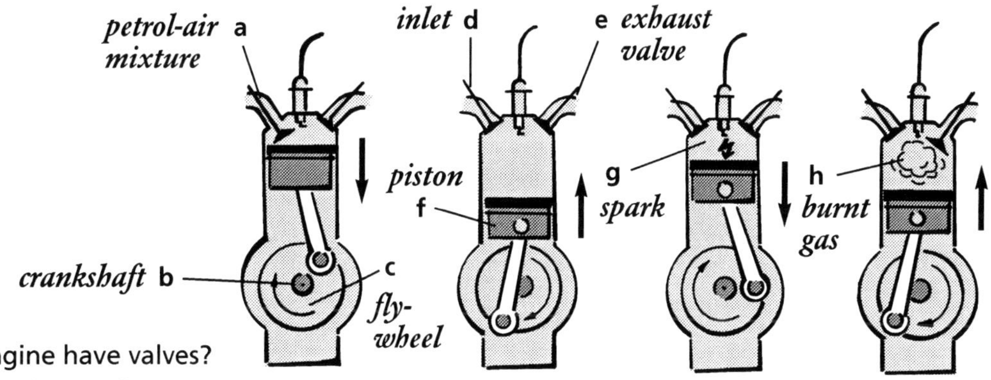

2. Why does the engine have valves?

To regulate the flow of gas and air.

3. What is the function of the spark plugs?

To ignite the petrol-air mixture.

4. Compare the movement of the piston to the movement of the crankshaft.

The piston moves the crankshaft which is the link to the transmission system.

5. Explain the changes that take place during the four-stroke cycle.

The piston moves up and down. The valves are opened and closed. Petrol and air are let in, compressed, and let out.

6. Find the right term first, then complete the text below.
(watch the correct grammatical form)

1. press together = *to compress*
2. forced into the cylinder = *to suck in*
3. burning = *combustion, ignition*
4. devices that clean the car exhaust = *catalytic converter*
5. checking = *service*
6. checked, usually in a garage = *maintainance, service*
7. poisonous = *toxic*

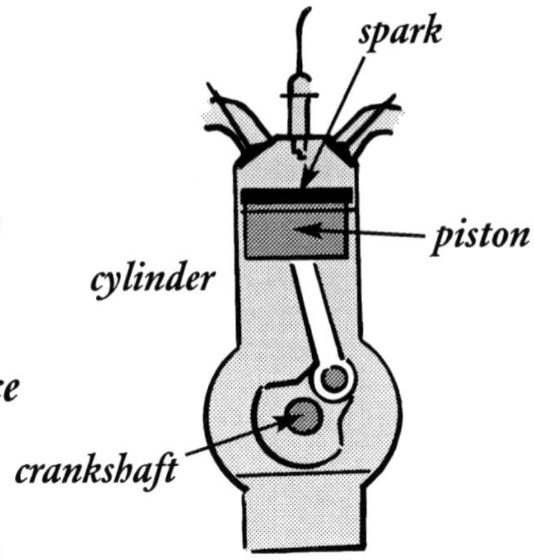

Diesel engines

In diesel engines pistons *compress* air to get pressures in the cylinders before the fuel is *ignited* : the combination of high pressures and temperatures is sufficient to cause spontaneous *combustion* without the need for *spark plugs* or a distributor. The process is very efficient and diesel engines produce only about 10 per cent as much pollutants as petrol engines with three-way *catalytic converters.* Petrol engines need frequent *maintainance* during their lives whereas diesel do not have to be *serviced* regularly.
That's the good news. The bad news is that the emission from diesel engines is very *toxic* .

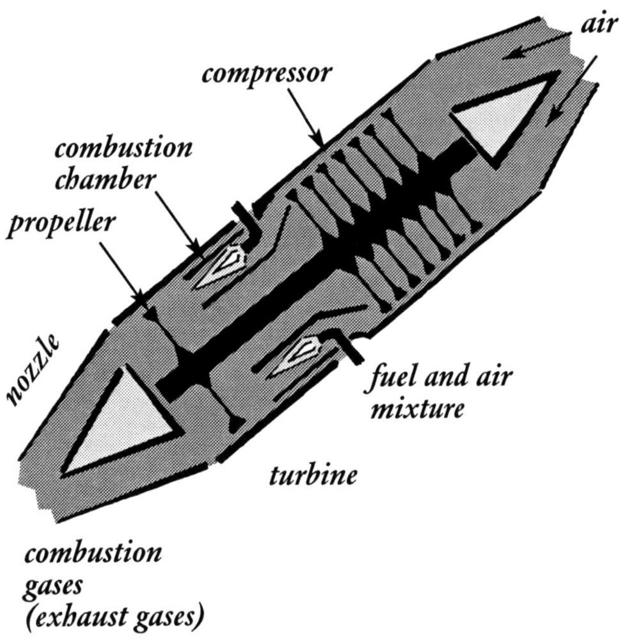

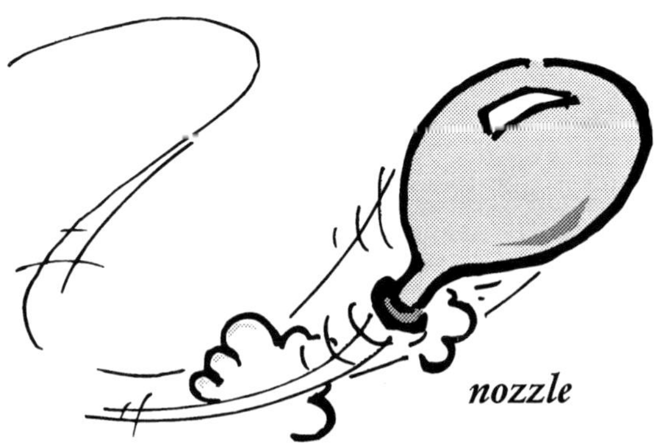

7. Label the two drawings above with these words:

fuel and air mixture, cylinder, piston, spark, combustion gases, crankshaft, propeller, compressor, combustion chamber, turbine, nozzle, exhaust gases

8. Use arrows to show the movement of air and gases. Then explain.

The motor effect

The wire in the drawing is between the poles of a permanent magnet. When current from the battery is flowing through the wire, there is a magnetic field around it. The wire and the permanent magnet repel each other and the wire moves upwards. If the current flows in the opposite direction the wire moves downwards.

The movement of the wire in the magnetic field is called the motor effect.

1. What happens when current is flowing through the wire?

There is a magnetic field.

2. Why does the wire move upwards?

Because wire and magnet repel each other.

3. When does the wire move downwards?

When current flows in the other direction.

---

2. Answer questions 1-6 in short phrases from the text.

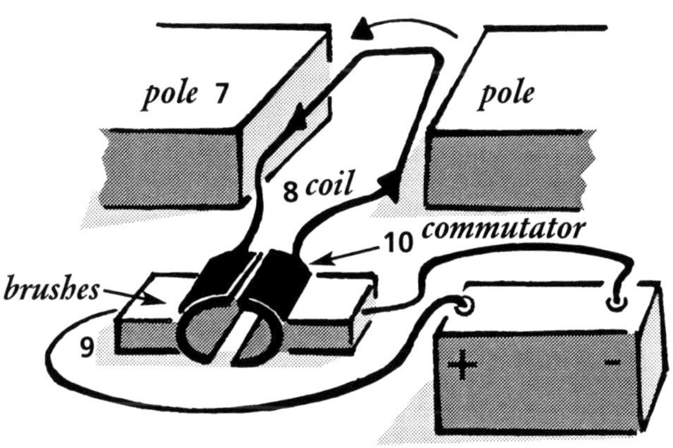

1. Using the words given in the text, try to identify the parts of this drawing.

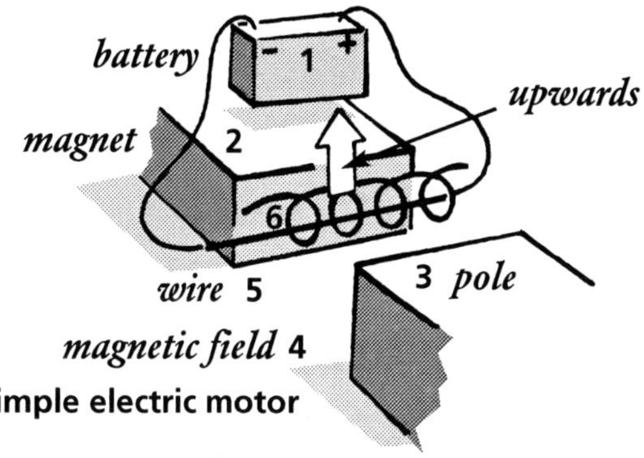

A simple electric motor

Electric motors use this motor effect. The simple electric motor consists of a coil which rotates between the poles of a permanent magnet. Because of the motor effect, one side of the coil moves upwards. The other side moves downwards, because the current there is flowing in the opposite direction. The coil rotates.

The direct current from the battery flows into the coil through brushes and a commutator. The commutator rotates with the coil, but the brushes do not move.

In this drawing there is only one coil and one commutator has only two segments. Normally the motor is much more complicated: there are many coils and segments and many motors do not use DC but AC (direct and alternating current).

4. Why does the coil rotate?

One side moves upwards, the other downwards.

5. How does the current flow into the coil?

Through brushes and a commutator.

6. What is the difference between this drawing and normal motors?

Normal motors are much more complicated.

3. Finally, finish these uncompleted sentences

1. From the battery current *is flowing into the wire.*
2. The wire is between two *poles of a permanent magnet.*
3. A magnetic field is *around the wire.*
4. The wire and the magnet *repel each other.*
5. The wire moves *upwards and dowmwards.*
6. From the battery current *is flowing through the wires and brushes.*
7. One side of the coil moves *upwards* the other side *downwards.*
8. The coil of the motor *rotates.*
9. The commutator *rotates* with the coil, but the brushes *do not move.*

Engines 4 – Electric motors   Lesson 2.7.2

Remember the new words?

Then this is a three minute exercise for you.

How an electric motor works

When you switch on an electric motor, it makes something ...*rotate*... . This could be the wheels of a toy train, for example. The electric current makes a wire which ...*coils*... inside the motor become magnetic. A ...*magnet*... then makes the coil turn, and this powers a shaft.

The electric current ...*flows*... from a battery through a coil which is between the ...*poles*... of a magnet. The coils produces a magnetic ...*field*... whose poles move towards the poles of the magnet. The north pole of the coil is attracted ...*towards*... the magnet's south pole. The south pole of the coil's field similarly moves towards the magnet's north pole. As a result, the coil ...*rotates*... .

As its poles pass magnet´s poles, the electric current suddenly reverses and flows in the ...*opposite*... direction. The commutator makes this happen. As the current reverses, the magnetic field does the same. The south pole becomes a north pole and the other way round, so that the coil is now ...*repelled*... by the poles of the magnet to which it was attracted before.

In this way, the coil keeps moving.

Don't forget!

AC	*Wechselstrom*
brushes	*Bürsten*
coil	*Spule*
commutator	*Kommutator*
current	*Strom*
DC	*Gleichstrom*
direction	*Richtung*
magnet	*Magnet*
magnetic pole	*Magnetpol*
to attract	*sich anziehen*
to drive	*antreiben*
to flow	*fließen*
to move	*bewegen*
to power	*antreiben*
to produce	*herstellen*
to repel	*sich abstoßen*
to reverse	*umdrehen*
to rotate	*rotieren*
to turn	*sich drehen*
to coil	*sich winden*
wire	*Draht*

1. *What are electric motors used for today?* – *Multiple electric devices in all walks of life.*
2. *What are the advantages of electric motors?* – *Pollution free, efficient, silent.*
3. *Explain advantages and disadvantages of electric motors in cars?* – *Antwort unter Zusatztexte Nr. 2 "Electric cars or hybrid engines?"*

Vehicles / Cars – A car cooling system

Most car engines are cooled by water. The water flows around the engine and then passes through the radiator. It then passes through the water pump and around the engine again.

FIG.1

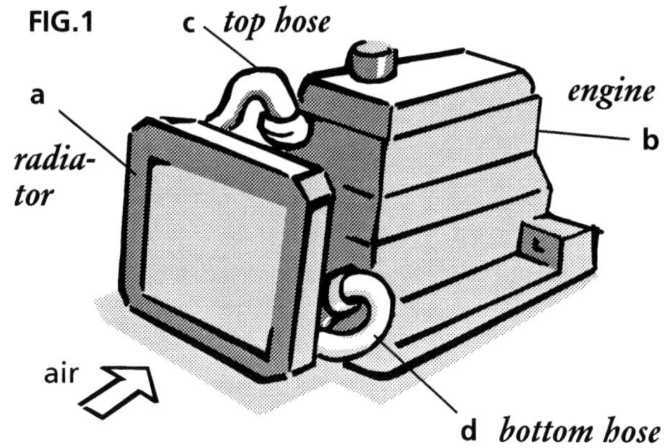

FIG. 2

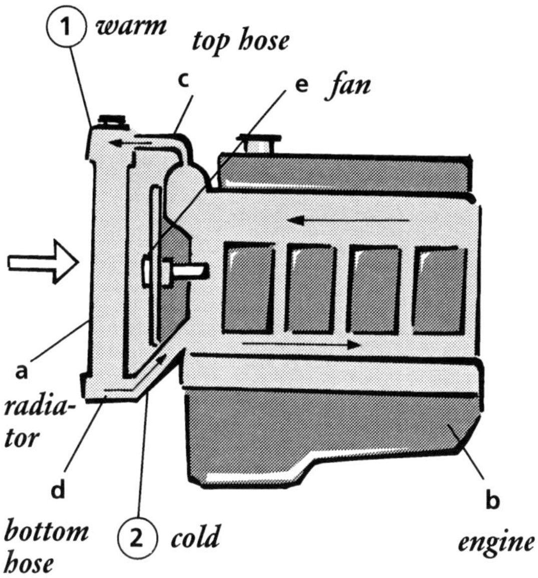

Here are the stages:

1. Water flows around the engine. The engine is cooled and the water is heated.
2. The hot water enters the radiator through the top hose.
3. It flows down through the radiator. Here it is cooled by air.
4. The cool water leaves the radiator through the bottom hose.
5. The water is pumped around the engine again.

Look at Fig. 3
Air is pulled through the radiator by a fan. This fan is turned by a belt, which is driven by the engine.

Look at Fig. 2
Is the water hot or cold at point 1.?
And at point 2?

FIG. 3

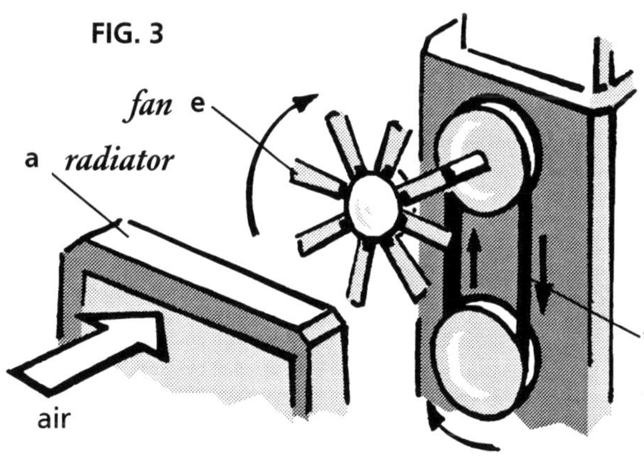

1. *What are the objects in the diagrams called?*

2. *Form correct questions and answer them.*

What

makes	the engine?
pulls	the water hot?
turns	the water cool?
drives	the water round the engine?
makes	air through the radiator?
pumps	the belt?
cools	the belt?

Option 2

Engines – How do gears work? – How do brakes work?

Lesson **2.7.**

Wie funktioniert ein Getriebe? **(Translation exercise)**

1. Das Getriebe ist Teil des Übertragungssystems. Dieses leitet weiter, bzw. überträgt die von dem Motor erzeugte Kraft auf die Autoräder.

2. Automotoren arbeiten am besten, wenn sich die Kurbelwelle ziemlich schnell bewegt. Dies geschieht immer dann, wenn das Auto mit hoher Geschwindigkeit fährt und der 4. Gang eingelegt ist (auch direkte Übertragung genannt). Wenn ein Auto langsam fährt, werden die Gänge benutzt um die Maschinengeschwindigkeit zu reduzieren, ohne etwas von ihrer Antriebskraft zu verlieren.

3. Die Kraft läuft über das Schwungrad zu der Kupplung, entlang der Wellen im Getriebe und schließlich zum Endantrieb, der mit den Rädern verbunden ist. Eine Anordnung von unterschiedlich großen Zahnrädern ist an jeder Welle angebracht und die Kraft wird durch diese übertragen.

4. Wenn der Fahrer den Gang wechselt, bewegen sich die jeweiligen Räder. Jeder Gang reduziert die Drehgeschwindigkeit und erhöht seine Kraft.

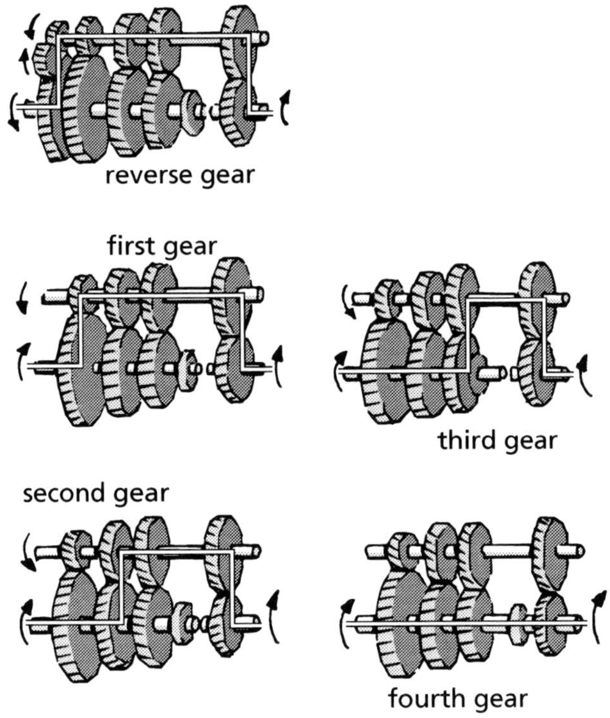

DISC BRAKES

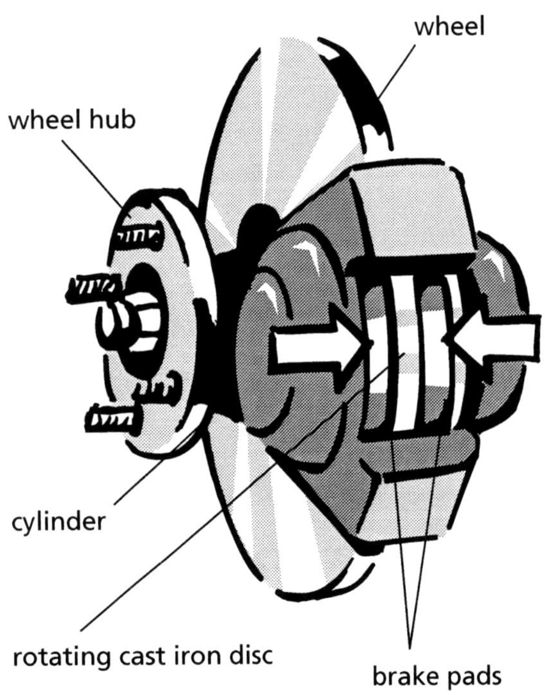

Wie funktionieren Bremsen?

1. Gute Bremsen sind sehr wichtig für sicheres Fahren. Der Fahrer benutzt die Bremse, indem er das Bremspedal nach unten drückt.

2. Moderne Autos haben Scheibenbremsen, wenigstens bei ihren Vorderbremsen. Wenn man das Bremspedal drückt, fängt der Bremszylinder an zu arbeiten. Gleichzeitig kontrolliert dieser anhängige Bremszylinder an jedem Rand. Die Kolben in jedem Bremszylinder pressen ein Paar von Metallkissen gegen eine Gusseisenscheibe, die die Drehbewegung des Rades stoppt.

3. Die Bremskissen sind der Schlüssel zu effizientem Bremsen und müssen stets in gutem Zustand sein. Sie müssen das Rad bei allen Temperaturen greifen.

4. Viele moderne Autos haben elektronisch verstärkte Bremsen, die den Druck des Fahrers auf das Bremspedal vergrößern.

5. Scheibenbremsen sind besser als die alten Trommelbremsen. In diesen pressen die untergeordneten Zylinder Bremsschuhe gegen die Bremstrommel, die dann die Räder anhält. Die Handbremse wird nur zum Parken verwendet.

Engines – Parts of an engine – Word field exercise

English	German	English	German
1 armature	*1 Magnetanker*	15 intake	*15 Einlass*
2 axis	*2 Achse*	16 jet	*16 Düse*
3 battery	*3 Batterie*	17 magnet	*17 Magnet*
4 bearing	*4 Lagerung*	18 manifold	*18 Einlasskrümmer*
5 belt	*5 Keilriemen*	19 nut	*19 Mutter*
6 bolt	*6 Bolzen*	20 piston	*20 Kolben*
7 bracket	*7 Klammer*	21 pump	*21 Pumpe*
8 bushing	*8 Lagerfutter*	22 ring	*22 Ring*
9 clutch	*9 Kupplung*	23 rotor	*23 Drehflügel*
10 coil	*10 Spule*	24 shaft	*24 Welle*
11 cylinder	*11 Zylinder*	25 spring	*25 Feder*
12 gap	*12 Spalte*	26 vacuum	*26 Vakuum*
13 gasket	*13 Dichtung*	27 valve	*27 Ventil*
14 ignition	*14 Zündung*	28 washer	*28 Unterlegscheibe*

E	E	P	Q	R	R	H	L	K	D	G	P	S	A	P	R	U
F	L	P	Q	E	O	C	C	P	C	U	X	E	A	J	V	L
L	R	P	H	L	M	T	U	X	C	T	S	G	H	Y	A	G
C	I	S	Z	B	W	L	O	E	O	S	D	P	M	S	L	D
T	A	O	R	K	L	C	B	R	R	J	I	S	R	K	V	D
W	G	E	C	E	S	G	Q	A	R	U	R	X	B	I	E	K
K	A	K	Y	N	D	U	G	I	T	T	T	R	A	B	N	B
P	C	A	U	O	E	M	N	N	L	T	A	A	U	W	X	G
O	Y	T	P	I	E	G	T	O	I	C	E	S	M	W	N	Y
I	L	N	I	T	G	O	B	I	K	R	H	R	S	R	P	R
N	I	I	S	I	N	O	S	E	E	I	A	M	Y	U	A	T
T	N	J	T	N	U	U	T	H	N	B	A	E	M	N	E	A
A	D	A	O	G	T	S	Y	G	R	C	V	P	B	J	G	J
C	E	K	N	I	U	T	M	A	N	I	F	O	L	D	J	X
M	R	A	A	A	J	J	E	L	T	T	O	R	H	T	Z	O
U	G	F	H	J	I	T	F	A	H	S	E	E	J	S	X	R
U	O	X	N	P	H	H	C	T	U	L	C	K	R	H	N	J
C	E	H	M	A	G	N	E	T	D	Z	J	D	S	I	S	J
A	S	O	L	E	N	O	I	D	A	X	N	Z	D	A	W	T
V	S	K	M	A	D	A	Q	A	B	A	X	A	X	O	G	R

there are more than the 28 items listed above

English	German	English	German
1 axis	1 Achse	*15 bearing*	15 Lagerung
2 battery	2 Batterie	*16 magnet*	16 Magnet
3 bolt	3 Bolzen	*17 armature*	17 Magnetanker
4 gasket	4 Dichtung	*18 nut*	18 Mutter
5 rotor	5 Drehflügel	*19 pump*	19 Pumpe
6 jet	6 Düse	*20 ring*	20 Ring
7 intake	7 Einlass	*21 gap*	21 Spalte
8 manifold	8 Einlasskrümmer	*22 coil*	22 Spule
9 spring	9 Feder	*23 washer*	23 Unterlegscheibe
10 belt	10 Keilriemen	*24 vacuum*	24 Vakuum
11 bracket	11 Klammer	*25 valve*	25 Ventil
12 piston	12 Kolben	*26 shaft*	26 Welle
13 clutch	13 Kupplung	*27 ignition*	27 Zündung
14 bushing	14 Lagerfutter	*28 cylinder*	28 Zylinder

1. Here are the four strokes of a petrol engine.

First, name the different parts in the drawing, next, explain shortly the different phases.

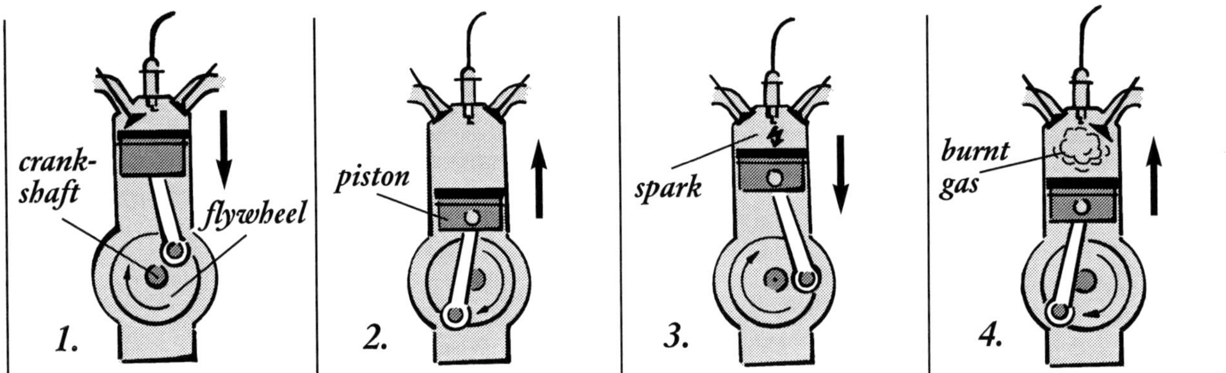

Intake Stroke	*Compression Stroke*	*Ignition Stroke*	*Exhaust Stroke*
– piston moves down	*– piston moves up*	*– piston moves down*	*– piston moves up*
– petrol and air is pulled into the cylinder through a valve	*– gas/air mixture is compressed*	*– spark plug ignites the compressed mixture*	*– exploded mixture is pushed out*
		– flywheel and crankshaft move camshaft	

2. Do you remember these parts of an electric motor?

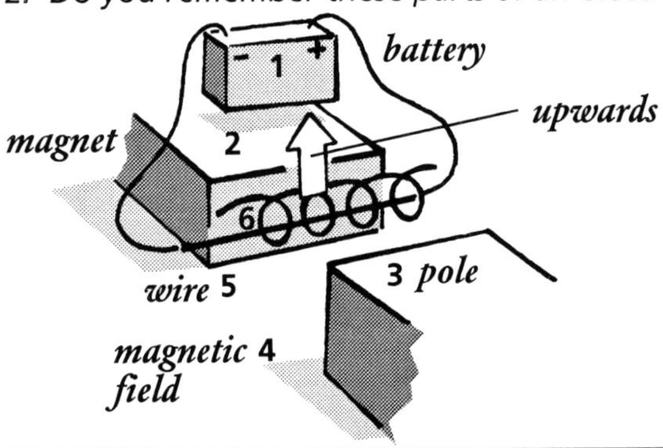

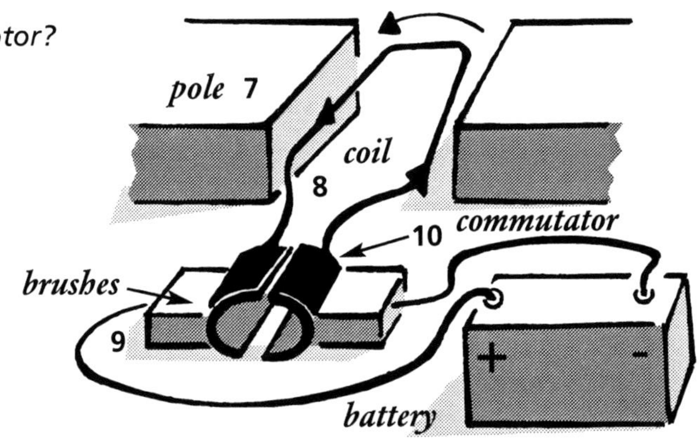

3. Right or wrong?

	Yes	No
1. Electric motors consist of a coil which rotates between two poles of a magnet.	X	
2. The coil and the magnet like each other.		X
3. There is no magnetic field around the coil.		X
4. Both sides of the coil move permanently upwards.		X
5. The coil between the poles rotates forwards and backwards.		X
6. DC flows into the coil.	X	
7. The brushes always stay fixed.	X	
8. You can use AC and DC for a motor.	X	

Vocab-check – Engines

Lesson **2.8.2**

1	axis	*Achse*	36	service	*Wartung*
2	beam	*Balken*	37	slit	*Schlitz*
3	bottom	*Boden*	38	spark plug	*Zündkerze*
4	brushes	*Bürsten*	39	stroke	*Takt*
5	camshaft	*Nockenwelle*	40	tiny	*winzig*
6	catalytic converter	*Katalysator*	41	tube	*Rohr*
7	coil	*Spule*	42	to allow	*erlauben*
8	combustion	*Verbrennung*	43	to be driven	*angetrieben werden*
9	commutator	*Kommutator*	44	to cause	*verursachen*
10	compression	*Verdichtung*	45	to combust	*verbrennen*
11	condenser	*Kühlrohr*	46	to complete	*vervollständigen*
12	crankshaft	*Kurbelwelle*	47	to compress	*verdichten*
13	current	*Strom*	48	to escape	*flüchten*
14	distributer	*Verteiler*	49	to expand	*ausdehnen*
15	emission	*Anstoß*	50	to fix	*fest machen*
16	exhaust	*Auspuff*	51	to ignite	*zünden*
17	exhaust valve	*Auslassventil*	52	to inject	*einspritzen*
18	flywheel	*Schwungrad*	53	to invent	*erfinden*
19	forerunner	*Vorläufer*	54	to propel	*vorwärts treiben*
20	fuel chamber	*Brennkammer*	55	to produce	*erzeugen*
21	ignition	*Zündung*	56	to release	*etwas loslassen*
22	inlet valve	*Einlassventil*	57	to repel s.th.	*sich abstoßen*
23	intake	*Einlass*	58	to rotate	*sich drehen*
24	jet	*Düse*	59	to spin around	*schnell herumdrehen*
25	magnetic field	*Magnetfeld*	60	to suck in	*einsaugen*
26	maintenance	*Wartung*	61	to travel	*sich bewegen*
27	nozzle	*Düse, Mündung*	62	to utilise	*benutzen*
28	opposite	*gegenüber*	63	top	*das Oberteil*
29	permanent magnet	*Dauermagnet*	64	valve	*Ventil*
30	piston	*Kolben*	65	washer	*Dichtungsring*
31	piston rod	*Kolbenstange*	66	wire	*Draht*
32	poisonous	*giftig*	67		
33	pole	*Pol*	68		
34	pollutant	*Schadstoff*	69		
35	pressure	*Druck*	70		

Computers 1 – Basic elements

How does a computer work?

1. Every computer consists of four basic units: the input, memory, central processing unit, and the output.
2. The keyboard is used to feed a new program of instructions into the computer.
3. Data and information are described by numbers.
4. These information are stored in the memory unit called RAM.
5. RAM stands for Random Access Memory.
6. The opposite of RAM is named ROM (Read Only Memory). This type of storage is used for data and information units which are used for running the system.
7. Both items form the memory unit.

terminal

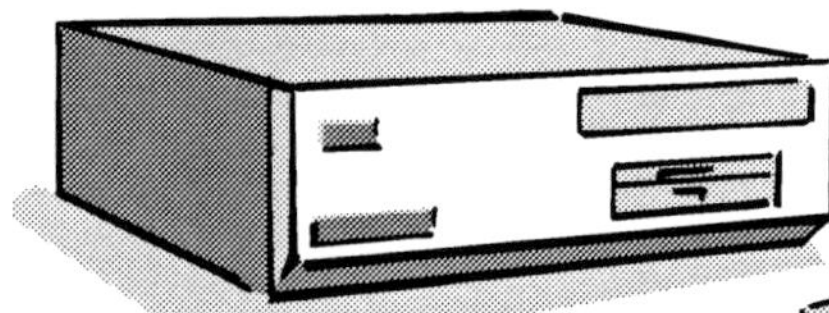

disc drive

disc

hand scanner

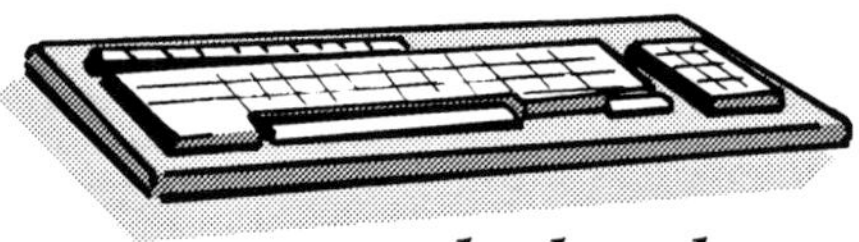

keyboard

mouse

monitor

joystick

writing pad

chips

printer

touch-on sweeen

plotter

Basic elements:

1	access	*Zugang*
2	bit	*Speichereinheit*
3	byte	*Speichereinheit*
4	capacity	*Leistungsvermögen*
5	cd	*Compact Disc*
6	delivery	*Ausgabe*
7	disc	*Disc*
8	drive	*Laufwerk*
9	hardware	*feste Computerbestandteile*
10	input	*Eingabe*
11	interface	*Schnittstellen*
12	joy-stick	*Joy-stick*
13	keyboard	*Tastatur*
14	memory	*Speicher*
15	modem	*Zwischenstück/Anschluss*
16	monitor	*Bildschirm*
17	mouse	*Maus*
18	output	*Ausgabe*
19	pad	*Matte*
20	plotter	*Zeichendrucker*
21	printer	*Drucker*
22	processor	*Rechner*
23	retrieval	*Verarbeitung*
24	scanner	*Einlesegerät*
25	software	*Software*
26	storage	*Speicher*
27	streamer	*Datensicherungsgerät*
28	terminal	*Terminal*
29	unit	*Einheit*

Computers 1 – Basic elements Lesson 2.9.2

Translation exercise:

1. Daten speichern
to save data

2. Informationen bearbeiten
to modify information

3. Texte übersetzen
to translate texts

4. Zeichnungen veranschaulichen
to demonstrate drawings

5. Berechnungen verändern und anpassen
to change and modify calculations

6. Probleme lösen
to solve problems

7. neue Maschinen entwerfen
to design new machines

8. falsche Berechnungen berichtigen
to correct false calculations

9. Daten verarbeiten
to process data

10. Informationen sortieren
to arrange information

11. fremde Daten einlesen
to scan strange data

12. Informationen speichern
to save/store information

13. fremde Situationen simulieren
to simulate strange situations

14. neue Räume berechnen
to calculate new spaces

15. Daten schnell verarbeiten und weitergeben
to process data quickly

16. Informationen sortieren und weiterleiten
to arrange and pass on information

17. Daten vervielfältigen
to copy data

18. virtuelle Räume entwerfen
to design virtual reality

19. Spiele simulieren
to simulate games

20. Texte verarbeiten
to process texts

Basic verbs:

1 to calculate	*1 berechnen*
2 to collect	*2 sammeln*
3 to correct	*3 berichtigen*
4 to create	*4 erschaffen*
5 to demonstrate	*5 veranschaulichen*
6 to design	*6 entwerfen*
7 to feed	*7 eingeben*
8 to function	*8 funktionieren*
9 to give out	*9 herausgeben*
10 to modify	*10 verändern, bearbeiten*
11 to multiply	*11 vermehren*
12 to process	*12 verarbeiten*
13 to produce	*13 produzieren*
14 to retrieve	*14 zurückholen*
15 to save	*15 speichern*
16 to scan	*16 einlesen*
17 to select	*17 auswählen*
18 to simulate	*18 simulieren*
19 to solve	*19 lösen*
20 to store	*20 speichern*
21 to translate	*21 übersetzen*
22 to arrange	*22 sortieren*

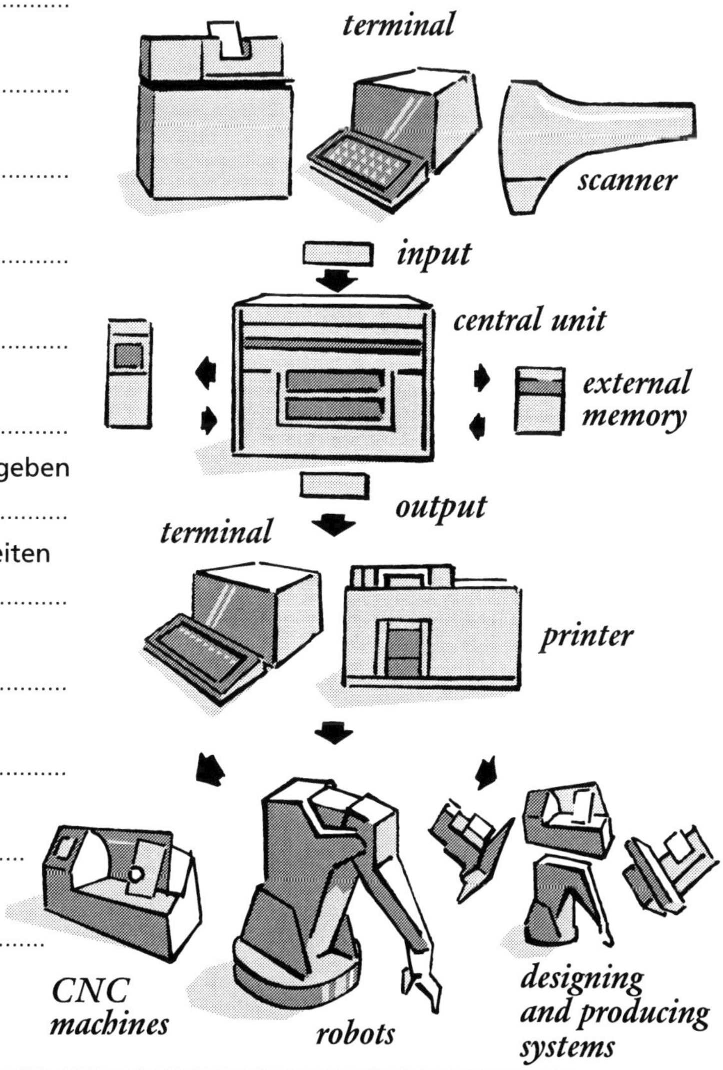

Computers 2 – New methods of production

Lesson **2.10.1**

Use of new computer technologies?

Complete the list.

Form sentences explaining the different items. – Beispiele Seite 70.

Car and traffic

air traffic control
anti-blocking-systems
board computer
(…)

Communication

broad-band technology
e-mail
fax, internet
satellites
fibre optic cables
(…)

Office and trading

calculator
videotext
typewriters
photocopier
telephone
(…)

Industry

Computer Aided Design
Computer Aided Engineering
Computer Aided Logistic System
Computer Aided Manufacturing
Local Area Network
(…)

Air traffic control
Anti-blocking-systems
Boardcomputer
Broad-band technology
Calculator
Camera
Clocks, watches
Computer Aided Design
Computer Aided Engineering
Computer Aided Logistic System
Computer Aided Manufacturing
Computer games
Computer tomography
Computerised Numerical Control
Computers
Cyber Space
Digital entertainment programs
Dryer
E-mail
Fax
Internet

Fibre-optic cables
Heating control
Local Area Network
Manufacturing Automation
Navigation system
Personal computer
Photocopying machines
Satellites
Sewing-machine
Solar energy
Storage control systems
Systems for auto-diagnosis
Telephone systems
Telex
Text production
Typewriters
Video
Video control
Videotext
Virtual Reality
Voice control

Medicine and architecture

computer tomography
systems for auto-diagnosis
video control
(…)

Energy and environment

solar energy
heating control
(…)

Household

dryer
heating control
personal computer
(…)

Entertainment and leisure

camera
clocks
computer games
cyber space games
digital entertainment
(…)

Computers 2 – New methods of production

Lesson **2.10.2**

	full expression	and in German ???
RAM	Random Access Memory	*Arbeitsspeicher*
ROM	Read Only Memory	*Betriebssysteme*
BIT	Binary digit	*kleinste Dateneinheit*
Byte	8 bits form one byte	*8 bits bilden ein byte*
CAD	Computer Aided Design	*Computergestütztes Konstruieren*
CAE	Computer Aided Engineering	*Computerg. Produktion u. Überwachung*
CAL	Computer Aided Logistic System	*Computergestützte Materialwirtschaft*
CAM	Computer Aided Manufacturing	*Computergestütztes Produzieren*
CAP	Computer Aided Planning	*Computergestützte Fertigungsplanung*
CAQ	Computer Aided Quality Assurance	*Computergestützte Qualitätssicherung*
CIM	Computer Integrated Manufacturing	*Computergestützte Fertigung*
CNC	Computerised Numerical Control	*Computergestützte Steuerung*
DNC	Direct Numerical Control	
LAN	Local Area Network	*Netzwerk zur Datenkommunikation*
LED	Light Emitting Diode	*Glühdiode*
MAP	Manufacturing Automation Protocol	*Schnittstellenarmierung*
OCR	Optical Character Recognition	*Standardisierte Schriftlesung*

In this section computer programmes introduce themselves. Find their correct names and put them in the right order.

I can do all the planning for new products.
CAP

I can do everything from planning to producing. *CIM*

I can connect all different computers in one firm and I also make an easy exchange of data possible. *LAN*

I can supervise and regulate the process of production. *CAE*

You need me if you want to find out more about the size, the shape, the look or the different parts of a new product.
CAD

I can plan the production methods. Tell you how much material and how many working hours you need. *CAM*

I tell you how much more material is available and where you find enough storage space. *CAL*

Computers 2 Lesson 2.10.3

	Erläuterungen / Arbeitsgebiete
RAM	**Random Access Memory** Speicher mit wahlfreiem Zugriff, Schreib- Lesespeicher. Mit RAM wird der Arbeitsspeicher bezeichnet. Es bedeutet der wahlfreie Zugriff auf die gespeicherten Daten, die man nach Belieben in den Speicher einschreiben und aus ihm herauslesen kann. Die Größe des Speichers wird in Kilobyte angegeben. Das Gegenstück zum RAM ist ROM.
ROM	**Read Only Memory** Ein Speicher, der nur gelesen werden kann, bisweilen unlöschbar, das Betriebssystem oder aber eingeschriebenen Hilfsprogramme für die Grundfunktion des Computers, etwa Tastaturabfrage, Bildschirmsteuerung oder ein Programm, das z.B. BASIC in die Maschinensprache übersetzt.
BIT	**Binary Digit** Ein BIT kann nur zwei mögliche Werte angeben: Null und Eins. Ein BIT ist die Kleinste vom Computer erkannte Dateneinheit. Alle Daten werden vom Computer in digitalisierter Form verarbeitet, d.h. sie sind vollständig als eine Kombination von 0 und 1 dargestellt.
Byte	**8 bits form one byte**
CAD	**Computer Aided Design** bedeutet computergestütztes Konstruieren. Der Konstrukteur oder Technische Zeichner arbeitet im Dialog mit dem Computer. An den Computer ist ein peripheres Gerät (z.B. Plotter) angekoppelt. Jede Veränderung in der Konstruktion wird vom Computer verarbeitet, optimiert und vom Plotter Schnitt- Detailzeichnungen, Perspektiven ausgezeichnet. (Besonders Automobilindustrie, Elektroindustrie, Maschinenbau). Das System kann ebenso Stücklisten, Arbeitspläne und nummerische Steueranweisungen erstellen.
CAE	**Computer Aided Engineering** umfasst den Einsatz von Datenverarbeitung in Produktion und Produktionsüberwachung. Dazu gehören Systeme zur Betriebsdatenerfassung oder Produktionskontrolle sowie flexible Fertigungssysteme (CAE oftmals mit CAP in CAM integriert).
CAL	**Computer Aided Logistic System** (Computergesteuerte Materialwirtschaft)
CAM	**Computer Aided Manufacturing** ist die Weiterentwicklung von CAD. Man versteht darunter das computergesteuerte Produzieren, das bis in die Funktion der Arbeitsvorbereitung, der Maschinensteuerung, der Prozesssteuerung, der Belegungsplanung, bis hin zur Werkzeugmacherei reicht.
CAP	**Computer Aided Planning** (Rechnergestützte Fertigungsplanung)
CAQ	**Computer Aided Quality Assurance** (Rechnergestützte Qualitätssicherung)
CIM	**Computer Integrated Manufacturing** (integrierte rechnergeführte Fertigung) bezeichnet den Versuch einer vollständig rechnergeführten Fertigung, bei der neben der mit CAD/CAM bezeichneten technischen Automation auch die dispositive Steuerung (Werkstattsteuerung) automatisiert wird.
CNC	**Computerised Numerical Control** bietet neben der Steuerungsaufgabe folgende Arbeitsbereiche: Programmierung, Speicherung, Kompensation, Diagnose, periphere Steuerung und Management Informationen, wie z.B. Betriebsdatenerfassung.
LAN	**Local Area Network** (Netzwerk zur Datenkommunikation innerhalb eines Betriebes)
LED	**Light Emitting Diode**
MAP	**Manufacturing Automation Protocol** Spezifikationsprotokoll für die automatische Fertigung stellt eine Normung der Schnittstellen für die Rechnervernetzung dar.
OCR	**Optical Character Recognition** OCR Leser dienen zur maschinellen Abfassung von standardisierten Schriften (Firmenausweise, Kreditkarten, Schecks, Zeitdatenerfassung).

Answers:

1. *The biggest difference is that there had not been a prototype before the plane was built.*
2. *The influence on the production process is that now the different parts can be designed and checked for their size and fittings before the actual production process. The checking process is very important because of the minute size of its components and the need to fit in perfectly.*
3. *The CIM (Computer Integrated Manufacturing) combines technical drawing (CAD) as well as computerized numerical control in the production process. In this way the whole production process can be controlled by the computer. In modern companies "concurrent design" means that designers and producers work together very closely.*
4. *The improvements are time, flexibility, accuracy and costs. The production time of technical drawings can be cut up to 90 %, alternations in the design can be made rapidly, the machines work extremely accurately, and the whole production process is very efficient.*
5. *Especially in car industries you find modern production technologies, though very often there still is a prototype because the models have to be tested for consumer's reaction. But in many other industries where machinery or electrical appliances are produced CAD and CNC technology have become an absolute must.*

1. *What is the difference between the new Boeing and formerly planned aeroplanes?*
2. *What influence does CAD have on the production process?*
3. *Describe how the CIM system works.*
4. *What are the improvements in integrated technology?*
5. *In which other industries have these new production techniques been introduced?*

Computers 2 – Language practise

Lesson **2.10.5**

1. Find correct expressions.
Klärung der einzelnen Begriffe sinnvoll.

random	only	design
computer	access	network
manufacturing	character	planning
read	digit	memory
local	automation	recognition
binary	area	protocol
optical	aided	quality assurance

Random Access Memory	*RAM*
Computer Aided Design	*CAD*
Manufacturing Autom. Protocol	*MAP*
Read Only Memory	*ROM*
Local Area Network	*LAN*
Binary Digit	*BIT*
Optical Character Recognition	*OCR*

2. Give internationally used English terms and short forms.

Comp. Aided Logistic System	*CAL*
Local Area Network	*LAN*
Computer Aided Design	*CAD*
Comp. Integrated Manufact.	*CIM*
Comp. Numerical Control	*CNC*
Comp. Aided Manufacturing	*CAM*
Random Access Memory	*RAM*

1. Computergesteuerte Materialwirtschaft
2. Netzwerk zur Datenkommunikation
3. Computergestütztes Konstruieren
4. Integrierte rechnergeführte Fertigung
5. Computerunterstützte Steuerung
6. Computergesteuertes Produzieren
7. Arbeitsspeicher

3. Look at this cartoon and try to find its criticism.

The machine forces man to give up individual personality and think in its systems and values only.

The categories of life are determined by technology.

„We're offering you the job on probation, Whitlock. You have three months to become one of us."

4. Are these statements right? If not correct them.

4.1. ROM is the storage system that you need to edit actual work.

No, RAM is the one that does it.

4.2. CAD means that you can only construct new machines with the help of a computer. If you want to produce these new items you must have another program.

correct

4.3. MAP means that you have only one program for production.

correct

4.4. CNC machines are programmed by specialists but cannot produce workpieces without the help of manual workers.

false (this statement refers to robots)

Option 1
Fibre-optic cables

Lesson **2.10.**

1. Glas cables carry messages at the speed of light. They have revolutionized telecommunications.
2. In 1988 the first transatlantic fibre-optic cable begins operating.
3. Its capacity of 40,000 simultaneous phone calls is three times as big as seven copper cables.
4. Optical fibres are used in medicine and engineering.
5. The loss of light from these early fibres was too great for long-distance uses.
6. Today, strands of glass are so clear that you are able to see through a block of it 20 km thick.
7. When light shines into one end of the fibre it is reflected 15,000 times per metre.
8. In multiplexing systems signals are sent in the gaps between other signals.
9. Another advantage of fibre optics is the minute size of the components.
10. The electrical transmitters and receivers used are so small that they could fit together in a matchbox, while the laser generators are no bigger than a grain of salt.
11. In future we can expect fibre optics to reach the individual house in so-called "broadband technology".

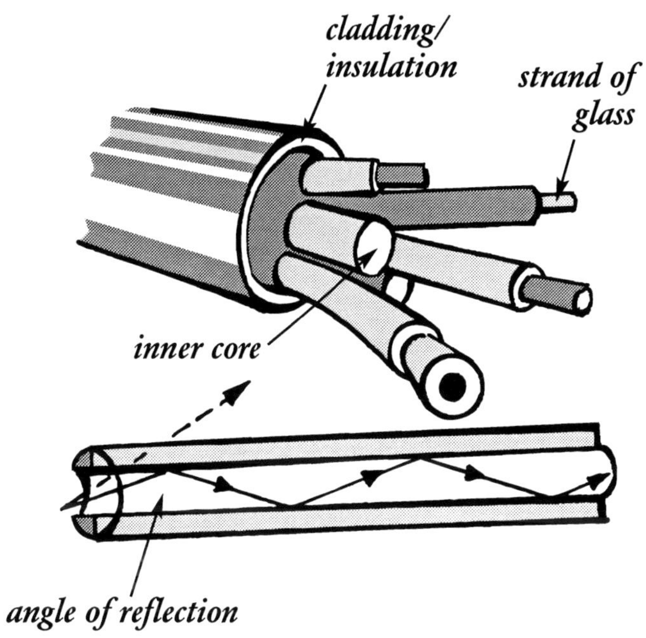

QUESTIONS:

1. What is the conventional material used in telecommunication cables?
   Normally copper is being used.
2. What material radically changes telecommunication?
   Fibre-optic cables made of glass are now being introduced.
3. How does "multiplexing" work?
   The gaps between the signals are used.
4. What can you say about the size of a laser generator?
   It is extremely small.
5. In what way are fibre-optic cables better than copper cables?
   Their capacity is much higher.
6. Name the parts of the fibre-optic cable.
   see above

Option 1
Fibre-optic cables

Lesson **2.10.**

TRUE or FALSE ???

	Yes	No
1. Copper wires carry messages at the speed of light.		X
2. The first transatlantic fibre-optic cable could carry three times fewer phonecalls than seven copper cables put together.		X
3. The loss of light from the early fibres was so great hat they were not used for long-distance applications.	X	
4. In future fibre-optical "broadband technology" will reach all houses.	X	
5. The (large) size of its components is an advantage of a fibre-optic cable. *small*	(X)	X

EXPRESSIONS

1. component	a.) single (item out of many similar ones)	*5. individual*
2. transmit	b.) spaces, intervals	*4. gaps*
3. application	c.) use (a material or method)	*3. application*
4. gaps	d.) send (e.g. radio signals)	*2. transmit*
5. individual	e.) any of the parts that together make a whole system	*1. component*

Which of these services do you think important in the future?
(Sätze mit "because" formulieren lassen)

- remote reading of meters for gas, water, electricity
- an on-line video library
- several different telephone lines per house
- computer networks for work from home
- up to 100 TV channels
- better quality radio in stereo
- high-definition TV
- computerized shopping and banking
- viewdata systems such as teletext
- video telephones
- burglar alarms linked to police station

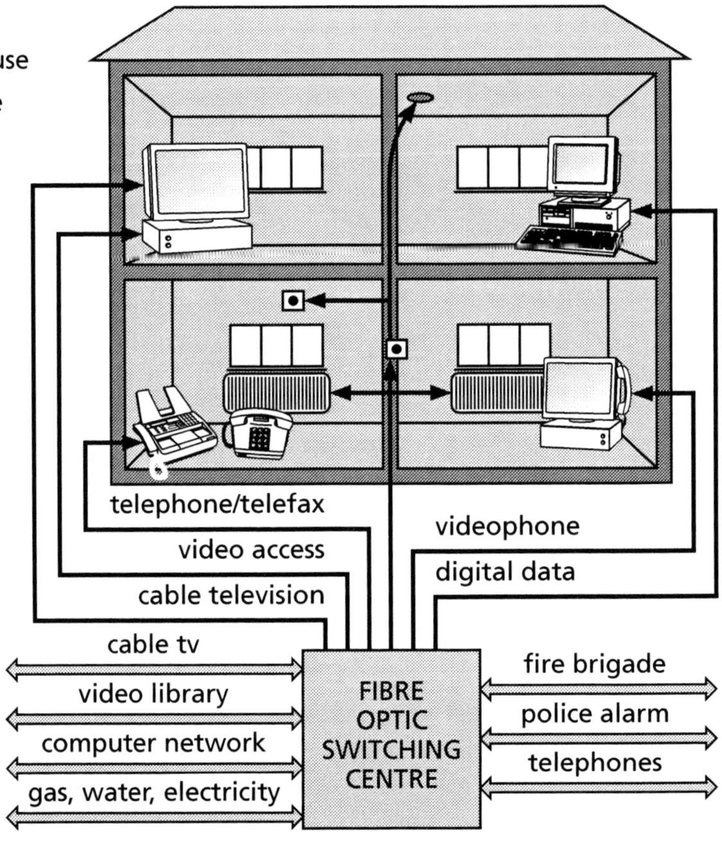

Additional reading:
Bill Gates
"The Road Ahead"
Penguin readers 1999
Chap. 8
"A home for the future"

Option 2
Computer memory – Use your dictionary
Lesson **2.10**

access = *Zugang* address = *Empfängerstelle* bank = *Reihenanordnung* batch = *Stapeldatei*
bit = *Speichereinheit* block = *Datenblock* cache = *Zwischenspeicher* capacity = *Kapazität*
cartridge = *Patrone* data file = *Datei* directory = *Verzeichnis* disk = *Scheibe*
drive = *Laufwerk* drum = *Walze* dump = *Ablage* fetch = *hervorholen*
field = *Rasterbild* gigabyte = *Fassungsvermögen/Kapazitätseinheit*

Useful information:

1. *Bits – basic units of memory representing in binary digits or bits.*
2. *Bytes and characters – eight bits form one byte, each character in a keyboard has its own arrangement of eight bits.*
3. *The ASCII code is the standard system for the binary representation of characters.*
   (ASCII = American Standard Code for Information and Interchange)

T	W	E	L	I	T	A	L	O	V	T	S	T	R	E	A	M
R	Z	T	B	I	Y	N	I	B	B	L	E	D	P	C	G	G
A	J	E	G	A	R	O	T	S	J	W	D	S	G	X	T	B
C	C	Y	T	R	K	S	S	S	A	O	O	I	E	I	C	N
K	B	A	J	I	K	N	A	S	F	C	T	N	K	R	E	B
L	C	G	C	G	B	M	A	E	E	V	C	S	H	G	T	Z
F	P	A	P	H	F	K	T	B	D	R	I	E	U	K	O	E
R	D	Z	R	I	E	C	C	R	B	D	D	L	S	I	R	M
R	J	A	E	T	H	Y	U	O	D	A	P	D	E	S	P	U
E	F	L	T	D	R	M	T	I	L	G	T	M	A	C	B	E
G	D	L	U	A	D	I	R	I	I	B	A	C	M	H	N	V
I	C	M	A	R	F	E	D	G	C	G	H	A	H	Z	Q	E
S	P	F	I	V	C	I	A	G	N	A	I	M	M	P	T	M
T	Q	V	L	T	E	B	L	E	E	L	P	E	O	Y	R	F
E	E	Z	O	D	Y	I	T	E	B	W	D	A	B	L	M	S
R	B	R	Z	T	I	I	R	O	Q	I	J	A	C	M	E	P
E	Y	F	E	V	C	G	X	T	A	S	G	O	X	A	M	K
U	Y	L	N	O	D	A	E	R	E	E	M	M	K	R	O	J
Y	Z	L	A	U	T	R	I	V	M	R	Q	S	T	J	R	C
D	P	Y	H	K	A	B	P	P	B	S	C	D	Q	V	Y	G

gulp = *große Datenmenge* magnetic = *magnetisch* mailbox = *elektr. Briefkasten* media = *Medien*
megabyte = *Kapazitätsgröße* memory = *Speicherung* nibble = *half a byte* protect = *schützen*
ram = *Arbeitsspeicher* read-only = *Systemspeicher* register = *Register*
reset = *auf Null stellen* retrieval = *Verarbeitung* storage = *Speicherung* stream = *Richtung*
track = *Spur, Rille* virtual = *vorgestellt* volatile = *flüchtig*

Revision Unit – Computers Lesson **2.11.1**

Basic elements	*1. Add suitable verbs.*	*2. Add a suitable item.*	**Basic verbs**
access	to have access to information	to calculate numbers	to calculate
bit	to store information in bit and byte	to collect information	to collect
capacity	*to have a big capacity*	to correct mistakes	to correct
cd disc	*to store data on cd*	to create new dimensions	to create
delivery	*to speed up delivery*	*to demostrate calculations*	to demonstrate
drive	*to install a drive*	*to design new items*	to design
hardware	*to improve hardware*	*to feed with information*	to feed
joy-stick	*to use joy-sticks*	*to function rapidly*	to function
keyboard	*to strike the keyboard*	*to give out data*	to give out
memory	*to extend memory*	*to modify processes*	to modify
modem	*to install a modem*	*to multiply the output*	to multiply
monitor	*to design flat monitors*	*to process data*	to process
mouse	*to click the mouse*	*to produce new designs*	to produce
output	*to select output data*	*to retrieve data*	to retrieve
printer	*to send commands to*	*to scan images*	to scan
processor	*to modify the processor*	*to select items*	to select
scanner	*to use the scanner*	*to simulate situations*	to simulate
software	*to improve software*	*to solve problems*	to solve
streamer	*to secure data with…*	*to store information*	to store
unit		*to translate texts*	to translate

3. Find correct expressions.

computer	character	control
manufacturing	only	design
optical	digit	memory
read	aided	planning
computer	numerical	recognition
binary	automation	----------------
computerised	aided	control

Computer Aided Design	*CAD*
Manufacturing Automation	*MAP*
Optical Character Recognition	*OCR*
Read Only Memory	*ROM*
Computer Aided Planning	*CAP*
Binary Digit	*BIT*
Computer Numerical Control	*CNC*

4. Give internationally used English terms and short forms.

RAM
input devices
CAP
storage/memory/saving
CNC
OCR
ROM

1. Arbeitsspeicher
2. Eingabegeräte
3. Protokoll für automatische Fertigung
4. Datenspeicherung
5. Computergestützte Steuerung
6. Optische Datenerfassung
7. Betriebssysteme, z.B. MS-DOS

Vocab-check – Computers D

Lesson **2.11.2**

1	Ausgabe	*output*
2	Bildschirm	*monitor*
3	Byte	*byte*
4	Datei	*file*
5	Datensicherungsgerät	*streamer*
6	Drucker	*printer*
7	Eingabe	*input*
8	Erkennung	*recognition*
9	Fertigung	*protocol*
10	Forschung	*research*
11	Geräte	*hardware*
12	Glasfaser	*fibre optic*
13	integriert	*integrated*
14	Kapazität	*capacity*
15	Laufwerk	*drive*
16	Lesegerät	*scanner*
17	Modem	*modem*
18	Nachricht	*message*
19	Prozessor	*processor*
20	Richtmodell	*prototype*
21	Schaltknüppel	*joy-stick*
22	Schnittstelle	*interface*
23	Speicher	*memory*
24	Speicherung	*storage*
25	Stapeldatei	*batch file*
26	Tastatur	*keyboard*
27	Übergabe	*delivery*
28	Unterlage	*pad*
29	unterstützt	*aided*
30	Verzeichnis	*directory*
31	wiederfinden	*to retrieve*
32	Zeichengerät	*plotter*
33	Zugang	*access*
34		
35		

36	ausstrahlen	*to emit*
37	auswählen	*to select*
38	beeinflussen	*to influence*
39	beinhalten	*to involve*
40	benötigen	*to require*
41	berechnen	*to calculate*
42	Daten eingeben	*to feed*
43	einlesen	*to scan*
44	entwerfen	*to design*
45	erschaffen	*to create*
46	funktionieren	*to function*
47	herstellen	*to produce*
48	hinein passen	*to fit*
49	lösen	*to solve*
50	sammeln	*to collect*
51	simulieren	*to simulate*
52	speichern	*to store*
53	übermitteln	*to transmit*
54	überprüfen	*to check*
55	übersetzen	*to translate*
56	verändern	*to modify*
57	verarbeiten	*to process*
58	verbessern	*to correct*
59	verdeutlichen	*to demonstrate*
60	vermehren	*to multiply*
61	zurückholen	*to retrieve*
62	zurückstellen	*to reset*
63		
64		
65		
66		
67		
68		
69		
70		

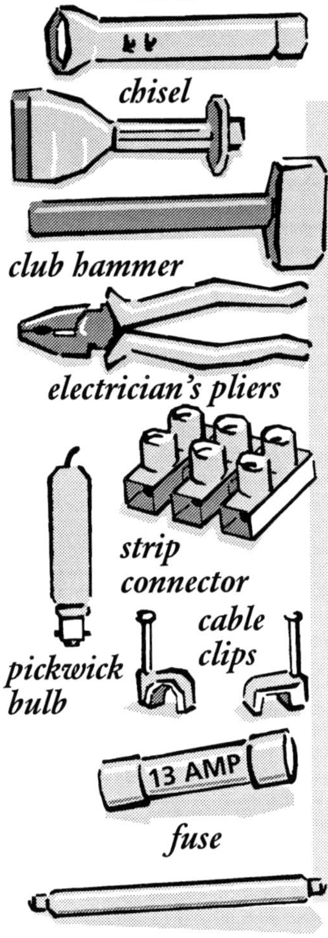

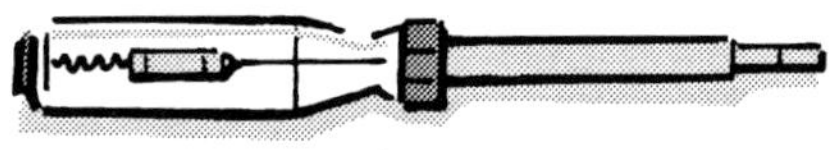

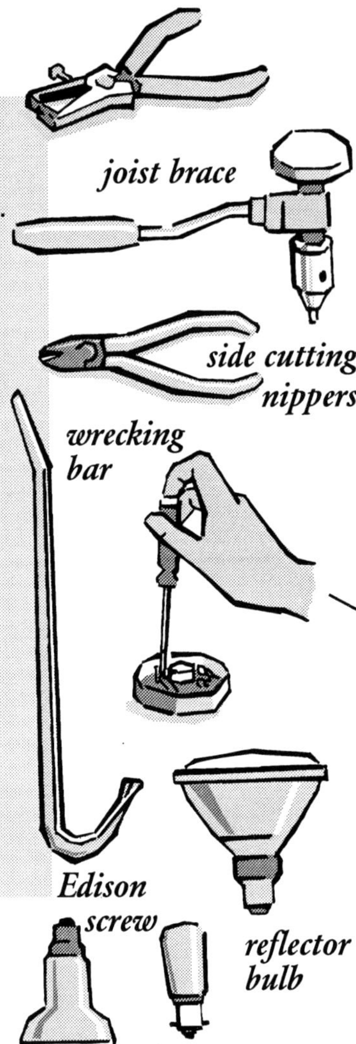

Electrical safety

1. Don't touch things, if you don't know them.
2. A wrongly wired circuit can kill.
3. Always use the correct size of cables
4. Conform to IEE regulations.
5. Always work back from the new circuit towards the live electricity source.
6. Double-check all your work.
7. Switch off the electricity supply before making the final connection.
8. Plan and do your work in daylight.
9. Never rush electrical work.
10. Always replace broken plugs and cables.
11. Follow instructions when wiring new appliances.
12. Never leave out earth connections.
13. Do not overload sockets with adaptors.

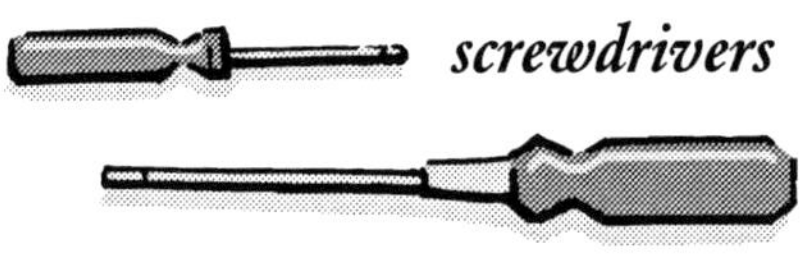

Electrical terms

AC/DC
Amps/Amperes
Gang
IEE Wiring Regulations
kWh
Ohms
Voltage
Watts

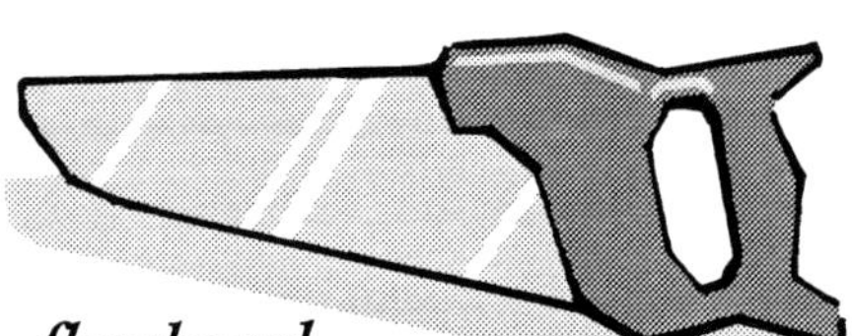

Can you identify these?

torch
strippers
neon mains tester
chisel
club hammer
floorboard saw
wrecking bar
side cutting nippers
screwdrivers
joist brace
electricians pliers
fuse
reflector bulb
striplight, bayonet cap
Edinson screw
strip connector
cable clip
Pickwick bulb

Symbols found on appliances

Double insulated
The appliance does not require an earth conductor.

Earth
Connect the earth conductor to this terminal.

L
Live
Connect the live conductor to this terminal.

N
Neutral
Connect the neutral conductor to this

Toolbox 1 – Electricity

Lesson **3.1.2**

1. Use the information given overleaf and give correct terms.

1. The Institute of Electrical Engineers guidelines for safe installation practice. *JEE*
2. With insulated handles these are used for cutting, bending and twisting heavy cable. *pliers*
3. Term for individual switches on a single accessory. *gang*
4. These are used for controlling the cut when stripping insulation from wires. *insulation strippers*
5. 76 mm and 178 blade length are useful. The smaller one is used for small terminal screws. *screwdrivers*
6. Available as strips of twelve. Cut off as you need them. Ratings: 5 amp, 15 amp, 30 amp. ~~*strip connector*~~ fuses
7. For cutting flexes and conductors. *side cutter*
8. Is used for drilling holes to run cables. *joist brace*
9. For using light when the mains are switched off. *torch*
10. For cutting channels in plaster to run cables. *chisel and hammer*
11. The measurement of elect. resistance. *Ohm*
12. The measurement of electrical pressure. *Amp*
13. For lifting floorboards and pulling nails. *wrecking bar*
14. The measurement of elect. consumption. *Watts*
15. Alternating and Direct Current. *AC + DC*
16. Measurement of electrical current. *voltage*
17. To test if appliances are live. *mains tester*

2. Using a mains tester. Put in the missing words.

With one finger on the metal ...*plate*... at the end of the handle, touch the blade ...*point*... on to a live terminal or wire. If ...*current*... is present, a neon lamp in the handle will ...*glow*... . A built-in resisitor ...*prevents*... shocks.

3. Somebody is making mistakes. Tell him how things are right. Use modals "can or cannot" and "must and must not".

1. I always use the size of cables that I like.
   You must always use the correct size.
2. I am not interested in IEE regulations.
   You must conform to regulations. You cannot neglect regulations.
3. I never make mistakes. I do not need control.
   You must double-check your work.
4. I am always in a hurry because I want to work a lot.
   You must never be in a hurry.
5. Sometimes I do extra work at night.
   You must not do extra work at night. You cannot do extra work.
6. Broken cables are not very dangerous.
   Broken cables can be very dangerous.
7. Using earth connections is only something for cowards.
   You must use earth connections.
8. If a plug feels hot, it must be a very hot and sunny day.
   You must switch off the current if the plug is hot.

Electricity supply

Lesson **3.2.1**

How is energy produced in a conventional power station?

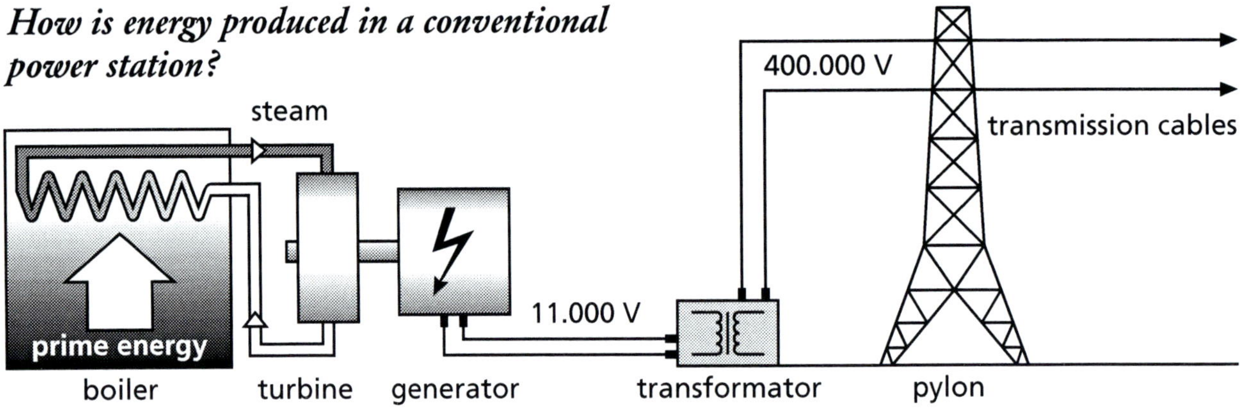

1. The electricity supply enters the house either by overhead or underground cables, passes through the Electricity Board´s main fuse and then to the Board´s meter.
2. From the meter it goes to the fused consumer unit. This can consist of either rewireable fuses, cartridge fuses, or miniature circuit breakers (MCBs).
3. From the consumer unit the supply is distributed throughout the house in the following ways.
4. One circuit passes under the ground floor, connects all ground floor sockets, and back to the consumer unit. This is known as the ring circuit or the main.
5. A second circuit serves the upper floor in a similar way. In a small house these circuits may be combined.
6. Lighting circuits travel to all the lights and switches via the roof and ceiling spaces.
7. Finally, individual radial circuits run to single, high consumption units, such as cookers, immersion heaters and instantaneous electric showers.

consumer unit fuses = NH Sicherung (Hauptsi...)

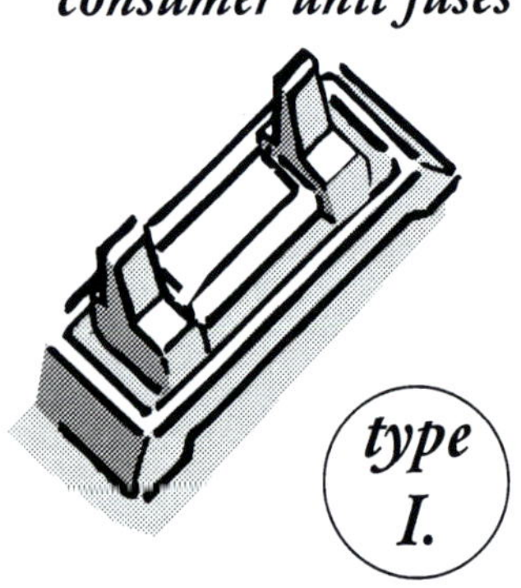

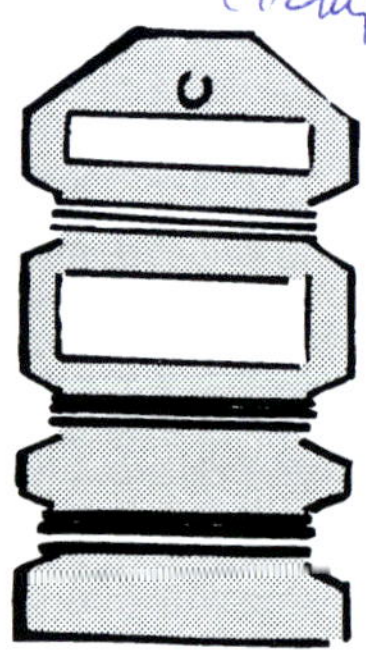

re-wirable fuse

automatic fuse

MCB

miniature circuit breaker

cartridge fuse holder

Kartuschebehälter ***normally used fuses***

Patron

Electricity supply Lesson **3.2.2**

Plugs:
easy plug, moulded plug, rubber plug, standard moulded plastic plug, plug adapter, rubber plug

plug adapter for connecting other plugs, too

standard plastic plug

moulded rubber plug (for power tools when plugs are likely to be dropped on hot floors)

easy plug (large ring moulded in-to the body of this plug for easier handling)

Sockets:
flush and surface socket, metal boxes, shaver supply socket, weatherproof sockets, co-axial sockets

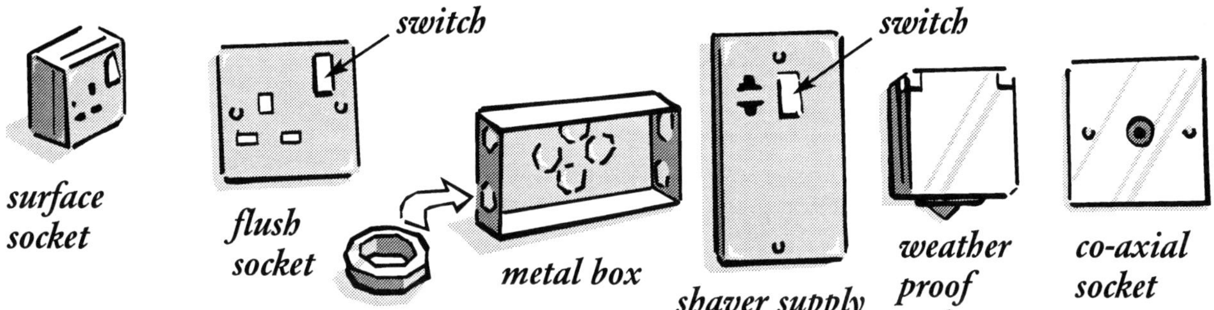

surface socket

flush socket

metal box

shaver supply socket (different voltage in GB overload device, restrictive power)

weather proof socket

co-axial socket

Switches:
torpedo switch, dimmer switch

single switch

double switch

torpedo switch

dimmer switches

Cables and flexes:

Live	*brown*
Earth	*yellow/green*
Neutral	*blue*

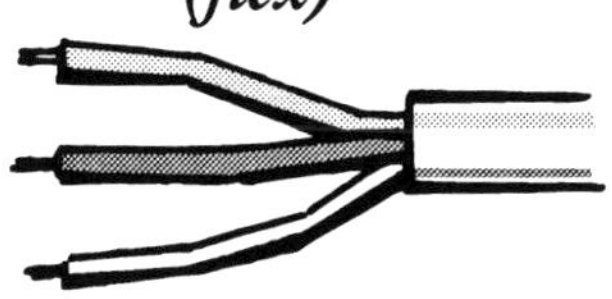

Live	*red*
Earth	*bare*
Neutral	*black*

Cable is used for fixed installations throughout the house. Flex is used to connect movable appliances to sockets, and light fittings to ceiling roses, etc. Cable and flex is designated by the cross section of the copper conductors (wires). It is sold by the meter from most DIY outlets. For large jobs, 50m and 100m drums are available.

Electricity supply

Lesson **3.2.3**

Look at the diagram of the circu

1. First, spot these items:

mains switch
meter
pump
hi-fi
cable drum
surface socket
bulb
switch
standard moulded plug
cables

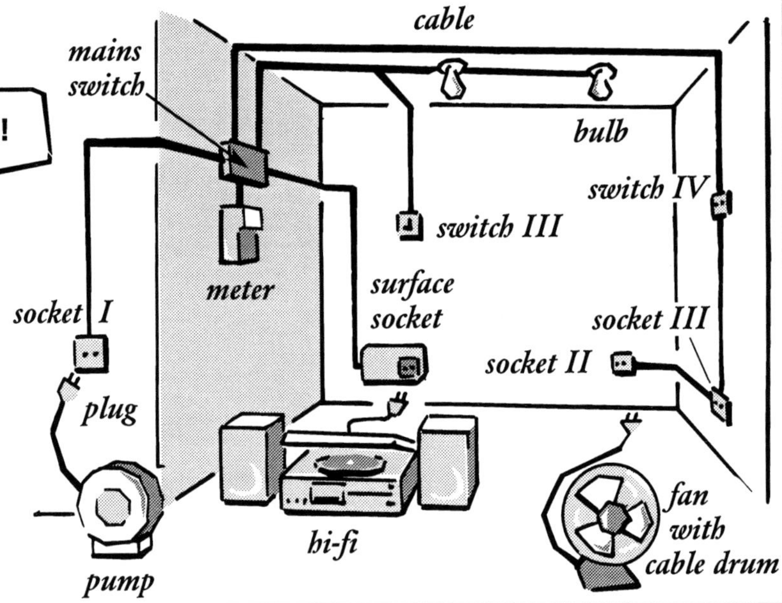

2. Describe how electric current is travelling through the cables to the various appliances.

Current travels through the meter to the mains switch.

From there it flows to sockets and switches.

Socket I is used for installing a pump.

Socket II is used for a fan with a cable drum.

Switch III puts the light on and off.

Switch IV can cut the supply of current to the sockets II and III.

3. Now answer these questions.

1. You want to turn off the whole current. What do you do? — *You turn the mains switch.*
2. You want to switch off the ceiling lights. How do you do it? — *You press the switch.*
3. You want to operate the hi-fi system. How do you do it? — *You plug it in.*
4. You want to measure the flow of current. What do you do? — *You examine the meter.*
5. You want to turn on the pump. How do you do it? — *You insert the plug.*
6. You want to switch the fan on. How do you do it? — *You put the plug into Socket Nr. II.*

Here are some verbs that might help you:
to press up, to insert, to push up, to put into, to plug in, to examine, to unplug, to switch on, to switch off, to turn up, to turn down

Option 1

Electrical repairs

Lesson **3.2.4**

1. You must always ***switch*** off the electricity before you start to do any electrical repairs. If you want to fit a new light you should check the ***wires*** in the ceiling. They are attached to a ***terminal block*** with two ***clamps*** for each wire. You must loosen the tiny screws in the terminal block, ***strip*** the ***sheathing*** off the ends of the wires, put the ends in the terminal block and tighten the ***screws*** again. Make sure that there are no loose strands of wire touching. You must put a bulb in and ***switch on*** the ***light***. Hopefully it works. If not, check the ***bulb***, the ***fuse***, or the connections in your terminal block.

2. Find the names in the above text.

to fit
to check
to be attached to
to loosen
to strip
to tighten
to make sure

loose strands
sheating
terminal block

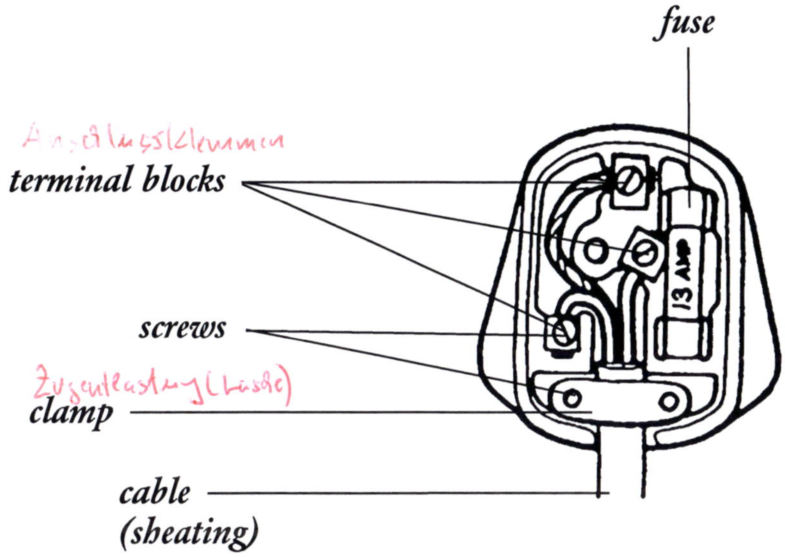

3. Some more words from the text dealing with electricity.

3.1. ***st*** r ***ip***
3.2. ***s*** c ***rews***
3.3. ***she*** a ***ting***
3.4. ***swi*** t ***ch on***
3.5. ***wi*** r ***es***
3.6. ***ele*** c ***tri*** c ***al***
3.7. b ***ulb***
3.8. ***clamp*** s
3.9. t ***erminal block***
3.10. ***ligh*** t

4. Rick and Jason at work

Rick:	Jason, you must switch off the electricity.
Jason:	Can't I do this without switching the electricity off?
Rick:	No, you can´t. Otherwise you´ll all blow us up.
	Do you need a screwdriver for your repair?
Jason:	Oh yes, thank you.

Option 1

Electrical repairs

Lesson **3.2.5**

Fill in the missing modals.

Rick: ....*Can*........ I switch on the electricity at the mains before I start fixing this lamp?

Jason: No, you ....*can't*........, it's dangerous. You ....*mustn't*........ do any repairs with the power on.

Rick: Yes, I see. ....*Must*........ I check the wires in the ceiling?

Jason: Yes, you ....*must*........ .

Rick: ....*Must*........ I attach the wires to the terminal block with two clamps?

Jason: Don't ask stupid questions. This is what you ....*have*........ to do.
And you ....*must*........ loosen the tiny screws in the terminal block,
and you ....*must*........ strip the sheathing off the ends, before you connect them, clear?

Rick: Don't play the boss all the time. I know what I ....*have*........ to do.
What about the ends in the terminal block?

Jason: You ....*must*........ (not) leave strands of wire. You ....*have to*........ make sure that there are no loose strands of wire touching.

Rick: OK, super boss, how come you are so bloody clever?

can
cannot
can't
must
mustn't
have to

5. Give instructions how to wire this plug.

1
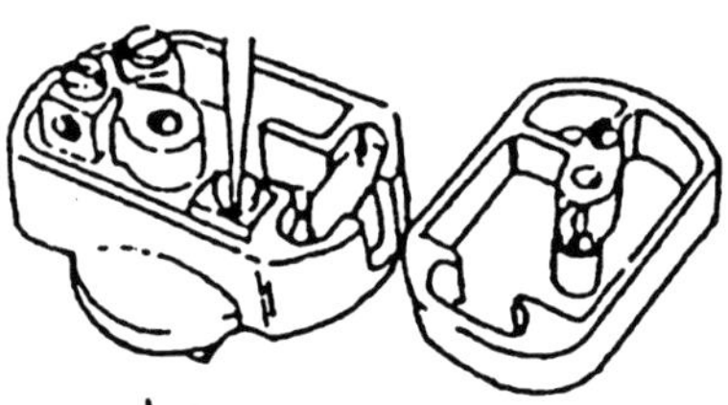

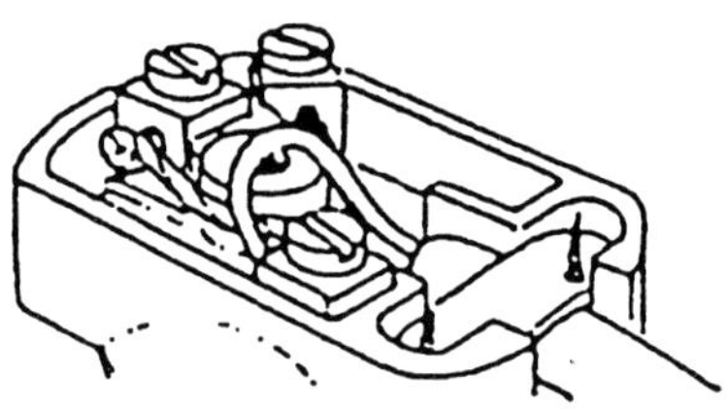
6

2

7

3

8

4
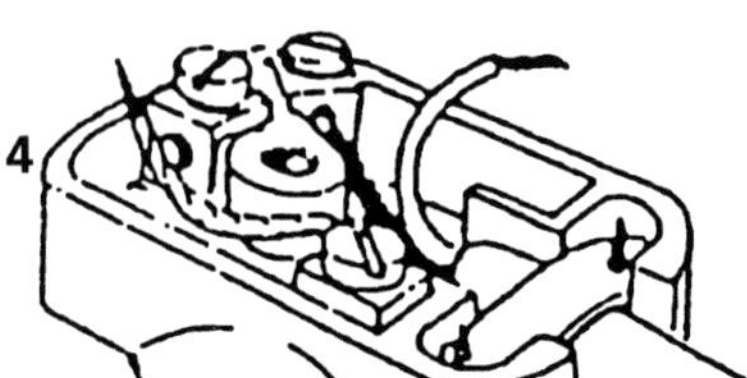

5

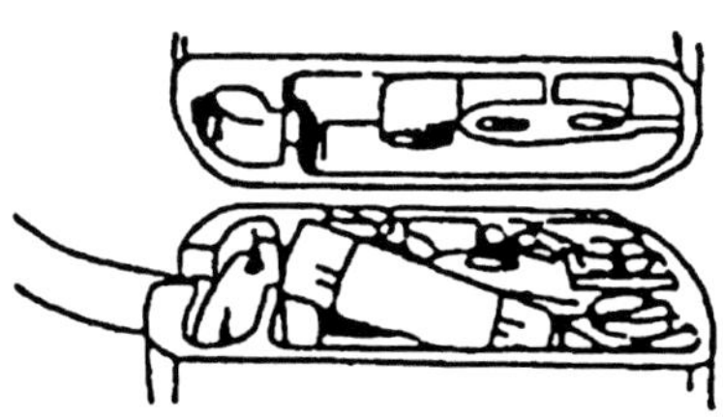
9

1. Loosen the screws.
2. Strip the sheating off.
3. Loosen the clamp.
4. Connect all wires to their correct terminals.
5. Make sure there are no loose ends touching.
6. Fasten the clamp.
7. Tighten the screws.
8. Check all connections.
9. Put the fuse in. Close the lid.

Option 2

How to ... – install a socket

Lesson **3.2.**

1. The recess and the channel are marked out with a pencil.
2. The plaster is cut away using a hammer and a chisel.
3. The brickwork is removed by drilling holes in it and then cutting it away with hammer and chisel.
4. The box is inserted in the recess and screwed into place.
5. The cable is placed in the channel.

FIG. 2

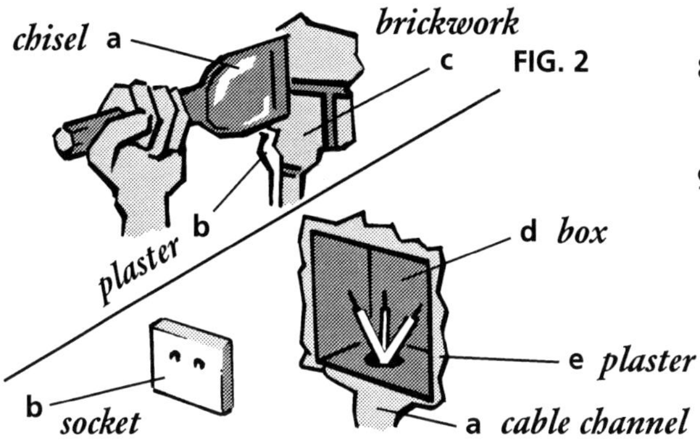

FIG. 1

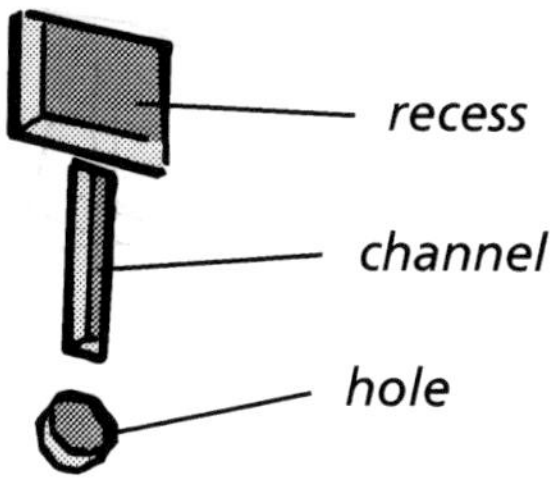

6. It is then pulled through the hole in the box.
7. The cable channel is covered. This is done by filling it with plaster, which is then painted or papered.
8. The socket is connected to the cable by inserting each wire in the terminal and tightening the screw.
9. The socket is screwed into the box.

FIG. 3

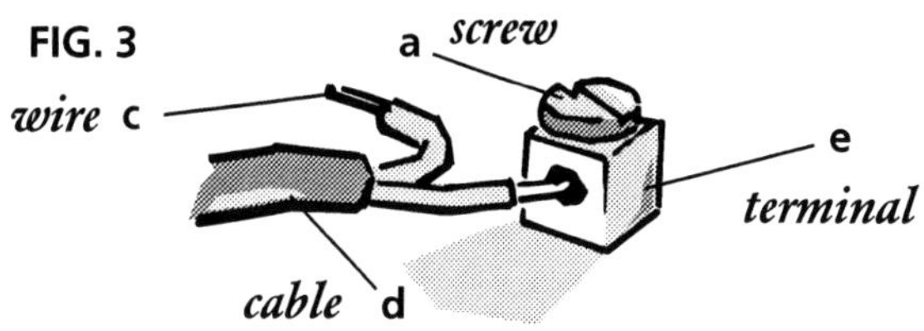

1. What are the tools in the diagram called?

Number a is called a chisel. Number **b** is called plaster. ...

2. Answer the questions.

2.1. What tools do you use for marking out the recess?

You need a pencil.

2.2. What tools do you use for removing plaster and brickwork?

You can use a hammer and chisel or an electric drill.

2.3. How do you remove the brickwork?

Drill holes into the brickwork, then cut it away with hammer and chisel.

2.4. What do you do after the box is in the recess?

It is screwed into place.

2.5. You place the cable in the channel. Then what do you put in the channel?

You fill it with plaster.

2.6. What do you put on the plaster?

Wallpaper and paint.

2.7. How do you fix the cable to the socket?

You insert each wire into the right terminal and tighten the screw.

Wie funktioniert ein Transformator?

(Translation exercise)

1. Ein Transformator verändert die Voltzahl eines elektrischen Stromes. Im Inneren des Transformators kommt der Strom in eine Spule und die Spule produziert ein magnetisches Feld. Dieses Feld bewirkt einen weiteren Stromfluss in einer anderen Spule des Transformators.
2. Ein Tranformator erhöht oder verringert die Voltzahl von Wechselstrom. Diese Art des Stromes verändert seine Strömungsrichtung mehrmals innerhalb einer Sekunde.
3. Transformatoren werden verwendet um Strom mit hoher Voltzahl für Langstreckenleitungen zu produzieren. Diese Spannung wird dann verringert in weiteren Transformatoren bevor sie die Haushalte erreicht.
4. Der Strom kommt in die erste Spule des Transformators, die ein magnetisches Feld in einem Eisenkern innerhalb der Spule erzeugt. Das Feld dreht sich jedes Mal, wenn sich der Stromfluss ebenso dreht. Es schneidet eine zweite Spule um den Eisenkern und erzeugt weiteren Wechselstrom in der Spule.

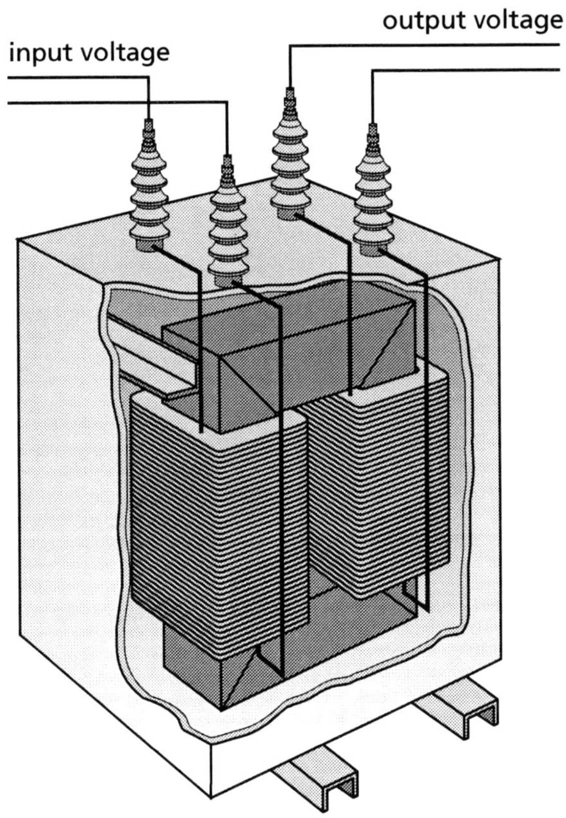

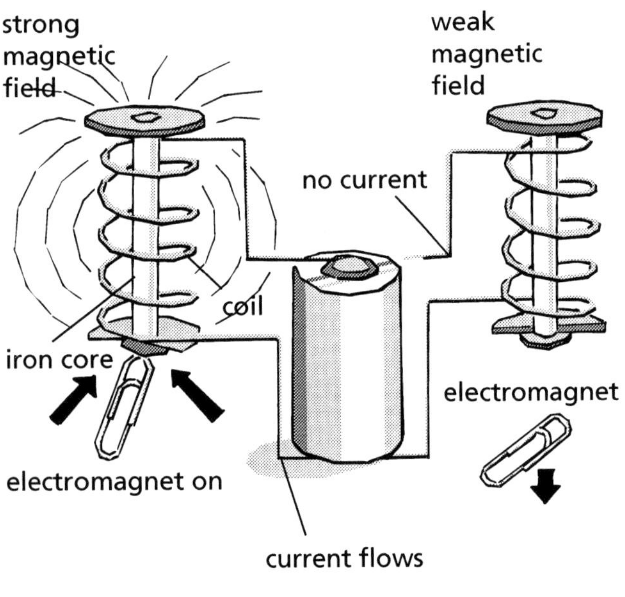

Wie funktioniert ein Elektromagnet?

1. Ein Elektromagnet ist ein Magnet, der durch Strom betrieben wird. Sein Magnetismus kann aus- und eingeschaltet werden. Er enthält eine Spule um eine Eisenstange. Wenn Strom durch die Spule fließt, wird die Eisenstange stark magnetisch.
2. Der Eisenkern innerhalb der Spule produziert ein viel größeres magnetisches Feld als die Spule alleine. Das kommt daher, weil die Spule im Moment des Einschaltens das Eisen magnetisiert.
3. Wenn der Strom ausgeschaltet wird, entmagnetisiert der Magnet sich sehr schnell.
4. Große Elektromagneten bei Kränen werden verwendet um Ladungen von Eisenschrott zu heben und zu transportieren. Der Elektromagnet hebt das Eisen im eingeschalteten Zustand und der Kran bewegt sich zu der richtigen Stelle. Dann wird der Strom abgeschaltet und der Eisenschrott fällt zu Boden.
5. Elektromagneten werden gebraucht um starke magnetische Felder in vielen elektrischen Maschinen zu erzeugen, eingeschlossen auch Motoren und Generatoren. Sie können ebenso verschiedenartige magnetische Felder erzeugen, abhängig von der Stärke des eingespeisten Stroms.
6. Elektromagneten werden deshalb in elektrischen Messgeräten, in Tonbändern und Lautsprechern verwendet.

Revision unit – Electricity   Lesson **3.3.1**

1. Translate into English.

1.1. Man muss immer die Spannung abschalten, bevor man elektrische Reparaturen beginnt.
You must always switch off the current before you start repairs.

1.2. Isoliere die Drahtenden ab.
Strip off the sheating from the ends.

1.3. Versichere dich, dass keine losen Drahtenden vorhanden sind.
Make sure that there are no loose ends.

1.4. Man muss die Schrauben festziehen.
You must tighten the screws.

1.5. Überprüfe die Sicherungen und die Anschlüsse.
Check the fuses and the connections.

2. Fill in the correct word and translate into German.

2.1. ......***Can***...... you tell him, which device is out of order.
2.2. You ......***can***...... measure high currents here.
2.3. ......***Can't I***...... have a new fuse?
3.4. You know what you ......***have to***...... do.
3.5. You ......***must***...... ......***not***...... leave some strands of wire.
3.6. These connections ......***must***...... be wrong.

can
have to
can't
must
must not

3. Name the following parts.

surface socket, switched

flush socket

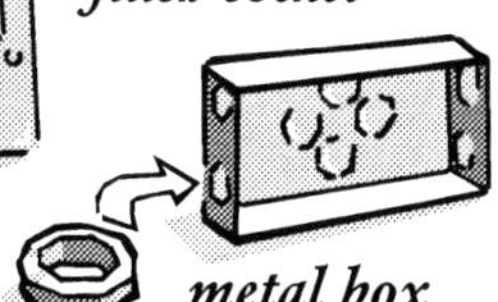
metal box

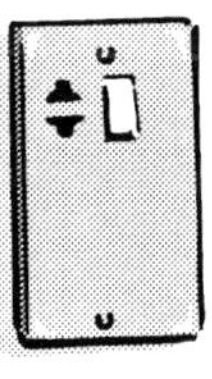
shaver supply socket

weatherproof socket

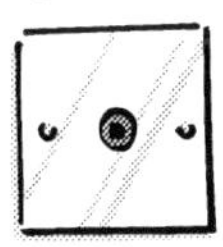
co-axial socket

switches

flush and surface socket, torpedo switch, easy plug, plug adaptor, dimmer switches, weatherproof socket, moulded rubber plug, metal boxes, co-axial socket, switches, standard moulded plastic plug, shaver supply socket

easy plug

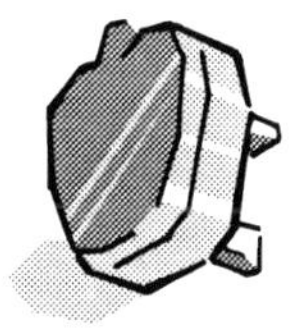

dimmer switches

4. Find the correct term for the following statement.

4.1. Outlet for tv or video arial. ***co-axial socket***
4.2. For connecting more than one plug to a single socket. ***adapter***
4.3. Cord mounted switch with rocker operation. ***torpedo switch***
4.4. The only socket allowed in the bathroom. ***shaver supply socket***
4.5. The standard way to connect moveable appliances to sockets. ***moulded plugs***

adapter

standard plug

5. Look for spelling mistakes. ***(7 mistakes to be found)***

Cable is used for fixed instalations througout the house. Flex is used to conect moveable appliancesto sockets, and light fittings to ceiling roses, etc. Cabel and flex is disigned by the cross-section of the copper condactors (wires). It is sold by the meter from most DIY outlets. For large jobs, 50m and 100m drumms are available.

Revision unit – Electricity Lesson 3.3.2

*6. Look at the drawing underneath, then name parts and explain their function.
Then tell your friend how to wire this plug.*

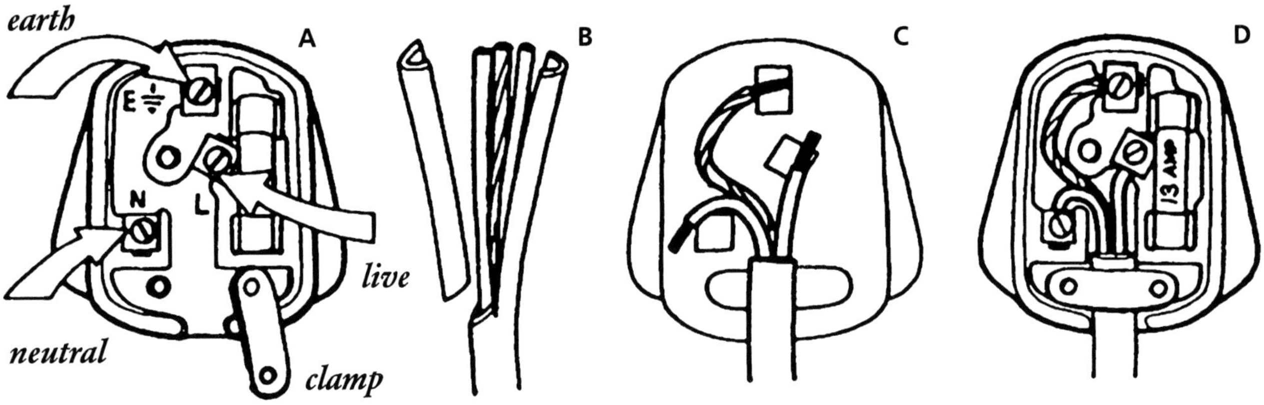

A. Remove the top and loosen one screw from the clamp.
B. Slit the outer sheathing lengthwise with a sharp knife.
Peel it back and cut it off away from the wires.
C. Use side cutters to cut the wires to length.
D. Twist the ends and secure into their right terminals.
Tighten the cable clamp.
Insert a fuse and replace the top.

Remember: green and yellow → earth
brown → live
blue → neutral

(oder gleiches Vokabular wie Übung 5, Seite 34)

7. Name these things by their correct terms.

1. With insulated handles they are used for cutting, bending and twisting heavy cable.
   electricians' pliers
2. Available as strips of twelve. Cut off as you need them. Ratings: 5 amp, 15 amp, 30 amp.
   fuses
3. Is used for drilling holes to run cables.
   joist brace
4. Term for individual switches on a single accessory.
   gang
5. These are used for controlling the cut when stripping insulation from wires.
   insulation strippers
6. For cutting flexes and conductors.
   side cuttes

8. Vocab check

torch, insulation strippers, neon mains tester, chisel, club hammer, floorboard saw, wrecking bar, side cutting nippers, screwdrivers, joist brace, electricians pliers, fuse, reflector bulb, striplight, bayonet cap, Edinson screw, strip connector, cable clip, Pickwick bulb

Vocab-check – Electricity

Lesson **3.3.3**

1	adapter	*Adapter*
2	appliances	*Geräte*
3	available	*erhältlich*
4	built-in	*eingebaut*
5	bulb	*Glühlampe*
6	cable channel	*Kabelkanal*
7	cable clip	*Kabelklemme*
8	cable drum	*Kabeltrommel*
9	circuit	*Stromkreis*
10	clamp	*Klemmschraube*
11	conductor	*Leiter*
12	connections	*Verbindungen*
13	consumer unit	*Verbrauchseinheit*
14	consumption	*Verbrauch*
15	current	*Strom*
16	device	*Vorrichtung, Gerät*
17	DIY	*Do it yourself*
18	electricity supply	*Stromversorgung*
19	fittings	*Passungen*
20	flex	*dünnes 3adriges Kabel*
21	flush socket	*Unterputzdose*
22	fuse	*Sicherung*
23	IEE	*(Sicherheitsbestimmung)*
24	insulated	*isoliert*
25	iron core	*Eisenkern*
26	live	*unter Strom*
27	mains	*Hauptschalter*
28	mains tester	*Spannungsprüfer*
29	meter	*Zähler*
30	mounted	*befestigt*
31	nippers	*Kneifzange*
32	outlet	*Auslass*
33	plug	*Stecker*
34	recorder	*Aufnahmegerät*
35	resistance	*Widerstand*

36	rewirable	*wieder verdrahtbar*
37	sheathing	*Isolierung*
38	socket	*Steckdose*
39	strips	*Streifen*
40	switch	*Schalter*
41	terminal block	*Anschlussstelle*
42	to attach	*befestigen*
43	to bend	*biegen*
44	to check	*überprüfen*
45	to connect	*verbinden*
46	to cut	*schneiden*
47	to distribute	*verteilen*
48	to examine	*überprüfen*
49	to fit	*einpassen*
50	to fix	*befestigen*
51	to insert	*etwas hineinstecken*
52	to measure	*messen*
53	to pick up	*aufheben*
54	to plug in	*einstöpseln*
55	to run cables	*Kabel verlegen*
56	to strip	*zerlegen*
57	to switch off	*ausschalten*
58	to turn down	*leiser machen*
59	to turn up	*lauter machen*
60	to twist	*drehen*
61	to unplug	*Stecker entfernen*
62	torch	*Taschenlampe*
63	wire	*Draht*
64		
65		
66		
67		
68		
69		
70		

Toolbox 2 – Metalwork

Lesson **3.4.1**

1. Try to identify the correct tools with the help of these words:

adjustable spanner (1)

open spanner (26)

socket spanner (21)

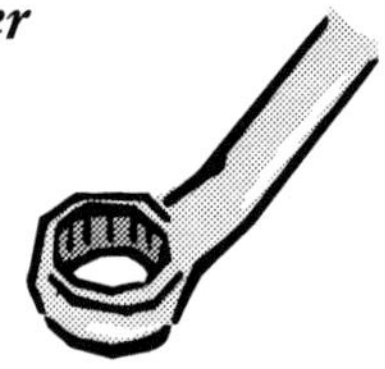

ring spanner (18)

nut and bolt (16)

circlip pliers (6)

English	German
1. adjustable spanner	*verstellbarer Schraubenschlüssel*
2. Allen keys	*Innensechskantschlüssel*
3. ball-pien hammer	*Polierhammer*
4. bench grindstone	*Bankschleifer (Schleifstein)*
5. bench sander	*Bankschleifer (Sandpapier)*
6. circlip pliers	*Sicherungsringzangen*
7. circular saw	*Kreissäge*
8. drill sharpener	*Bohrerschleifgerät*
9. drill stand	*Bohrständer*
10. files	*Feilen*
11. flexible drill shaft	*Schnellspannfutter*
12. grinding points	*Schleifköpfe*
13. jigsaw	*Stichsäge*
14. junior hacksaw	*kleine Bügelsäge*
15. mole wrench	*Gripzange*
16. nuts and bolts	*Mutter und Bolzen*
17. pliers	*Zange*
18. ring spanner	*Ringschlüssel*
19. rivet pliers	*Nietzange*
20. sawblades	*Sägeblätter*
21. socket spanner	*Steckschlüssel*
22. standard hacksaw	*Bügelsäge*
23. tinsnips	*Blechschere*
24. washers	*Unterlegscheiben*
25. wing nut	*Flügelmutter*
26. open spanner	*Maulschlüssel*

grinding points (12)

screw

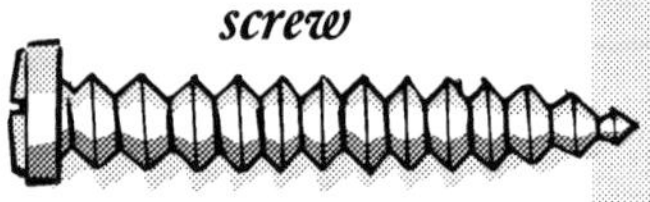

bolt

pliers (17)

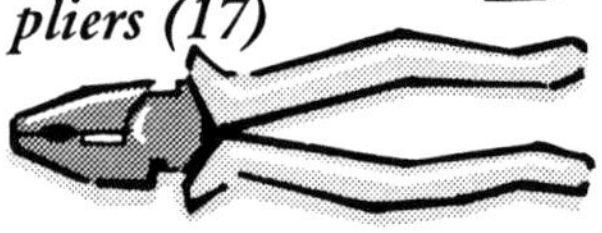

tinsnips (23)

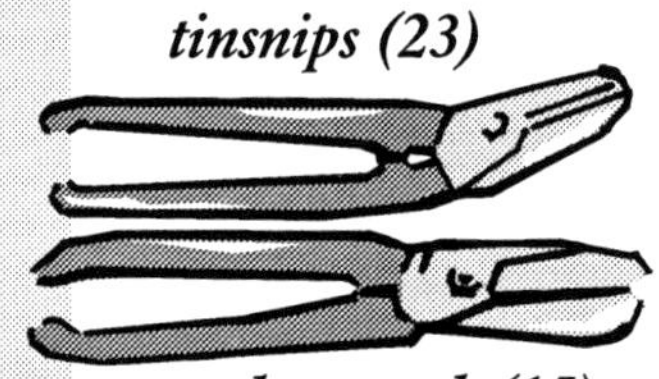

mole wrench (15)

junior hacksaw (14)

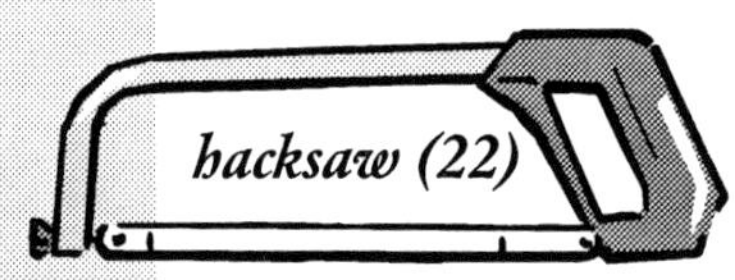

hacksaw (22)

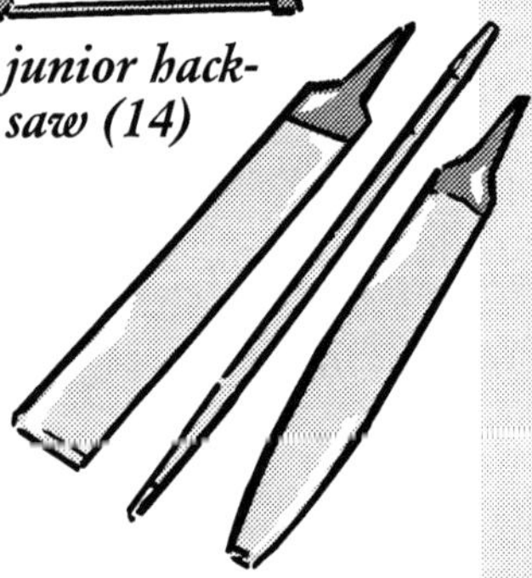

files (10)

Allen keys (2)

ball-pien hammer (3)

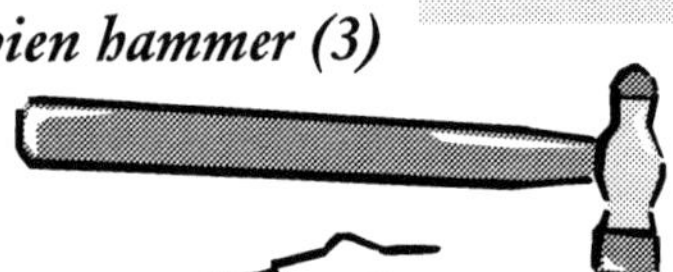

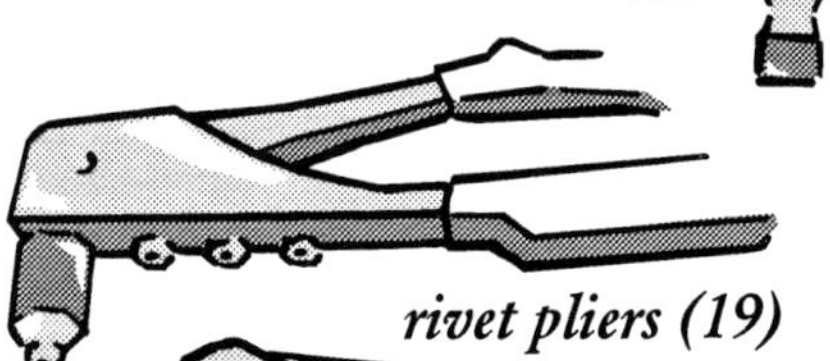

rivet pliers (19)

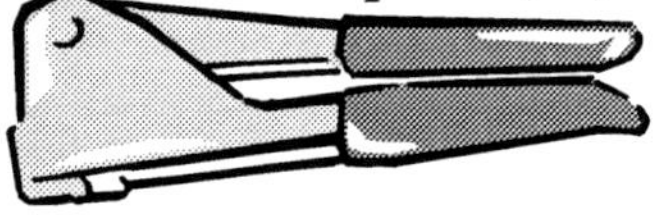

bench grindstone (4)

jigsaw (13)

Toolbox 2 – Metalwork Lesson **3.4.2.**

2. Name the correct tools or materials.
Then underline all verbs. How many different verbs can you find? ***(siehe Seite 70)***
(Bitte Arbeitsanweisungen auf S. 72 beachten.)

A	B	C	
This tool is normally used for cutting wood of all types. *circular saw (7)*	Used to do and undo nuts. Very handy because you can use this one for all sizes. *adjustable spanner (1)*	You use these pliers to join sheets of metal, particularly aluminium. Softer materials need a washer to strengthen the join. *rivet pliers (19)*	**1**
You can use this tool to cut all small bars of metal or loose ends. *junior hacksaw (14)*	A very useful tool around the house, because it can be used as pliers and can also clamp materials together and lock. *mole wrench (15)*	Found everywhere for joining metal components together. There are many various types of heads and threads. *nuts and bolts (16)*	**2**
Three basic types: flat, half-round and round. Various sizes available. *files (10)*		Available in a vast range of sizes. Used to spread the pressure over a larger area. Gives items an extra grip or prevents vibration. *washers (24)*	**3**
These little grindstones can be used in an electric drill or flexible drive for grinding shapes. *grinding points (12)*	For general metal working use. Head weights range from 100 g to 1,3 kg. 900 g is a good choice. *ball-pien hammer (3)*	An "L" shaped hexagon bar. Available singly or in a large range of sizes. Used for loosening or tightening Allen screws. *Allen keys (2)*	**4**
Special pliers for removing and replacing circlips. *circlip pliers (6)*		These you need for cutting of sheet metal, or curved for cutting left- and right-hand curves. *tinsnips (23)*	**5**
Standard frame. Takes 255 or 305 mm blades. Most are adjustable to take both. After putting in, turn adjuster for correct blade tension. *standard hacksaw (14)*	This machine has a fine wheel or a coarse wheel. Useful for sharpening cold chisels, screwdrivers etc. Be careful with overheating. Dip the blade in cold water frequently. *bench grindstore (4)*	These machines are smooth, powerful and quiet. They are safer than circular saws but take longer to cut. They can saw metal as well as wood. *jigsaw (13)*	**6**
For proper cutting make sure that at least three teeth are in contact with the material to be cut. Always fit blades with the teeth facing forward. *hacksaw blades (20)*	The type of spanner you use where access is limited. *open spanner (26)*	Usually bought in sets to cover a good range of sizes. Used with a ratchet handle. *socket spanner (21)* Nässe	**7**
An excellent cranked spanner which grips all around. *ring spanner (18)*	For removable fittings. Tighten or loosen by hand only. Comes in different sizes. *wing nut (25)*	This machine is used for sanding the end grain on wood or metal. It is driven by an electric drill on a work table. Replacements discs are available. *bench sander (5)*	**8**

Methods of welding

Lesson **3.5.1**

Welding is the joining of metals by fusion.

Complete the drawings by putting in the appropriate words from the list below.

Form sentences with the appropriate nouns and verbs.

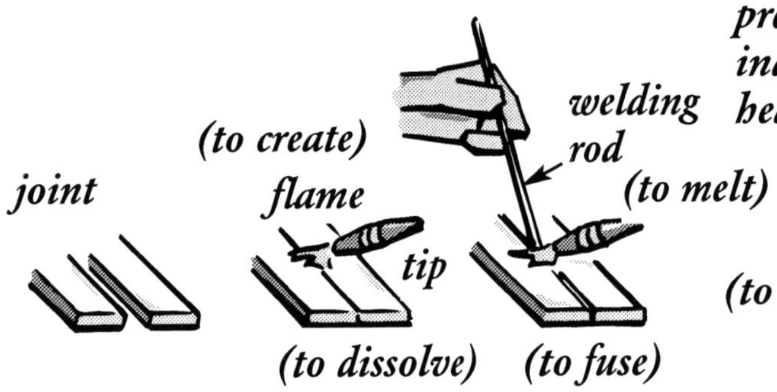

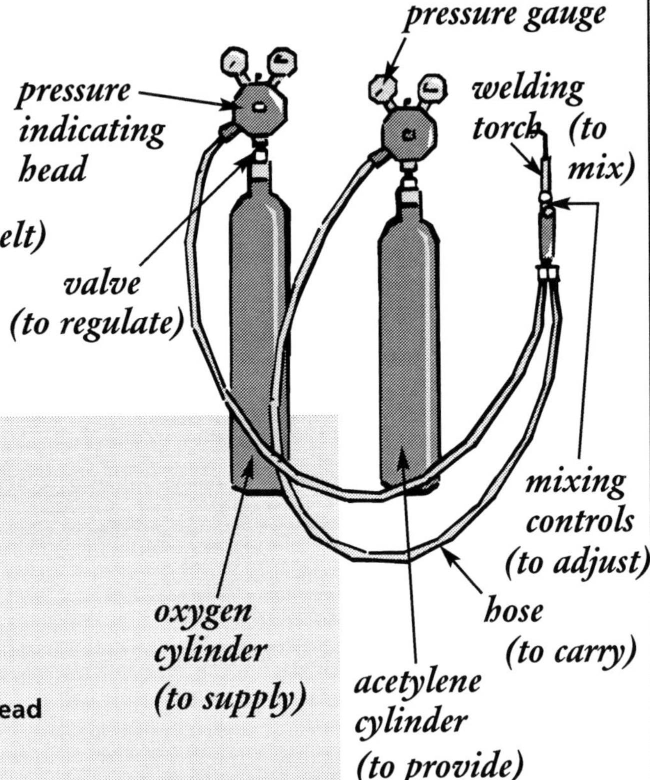

1. switch
2. transformer
3. cables
4. pressure gauge
5. acetylene cylinder
6. welding torch
7. pressure indicating head
8. mixing controls
9. plug
10. earth clamp
11. welding electrode
12. hoses
13. electrode holder
14. valve

15. to fuse, to adjust, to carry, to be attached, to regulate, to melt, to operate, to overheat, to protect, to supply, to dissolve, to mix, to create, to provide

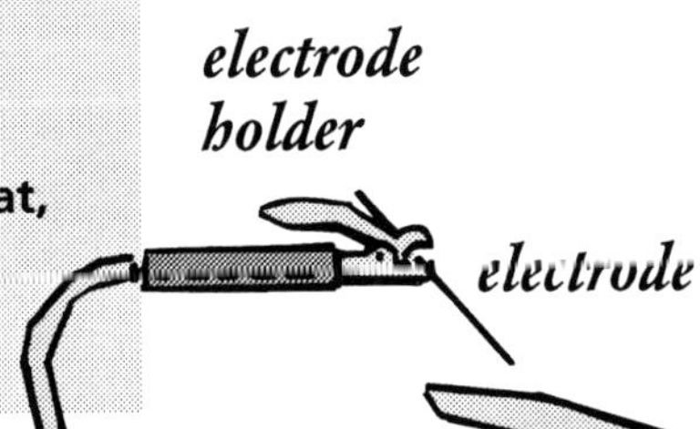

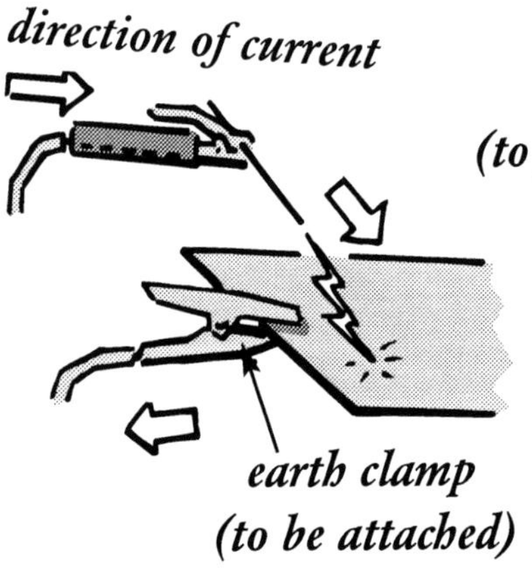

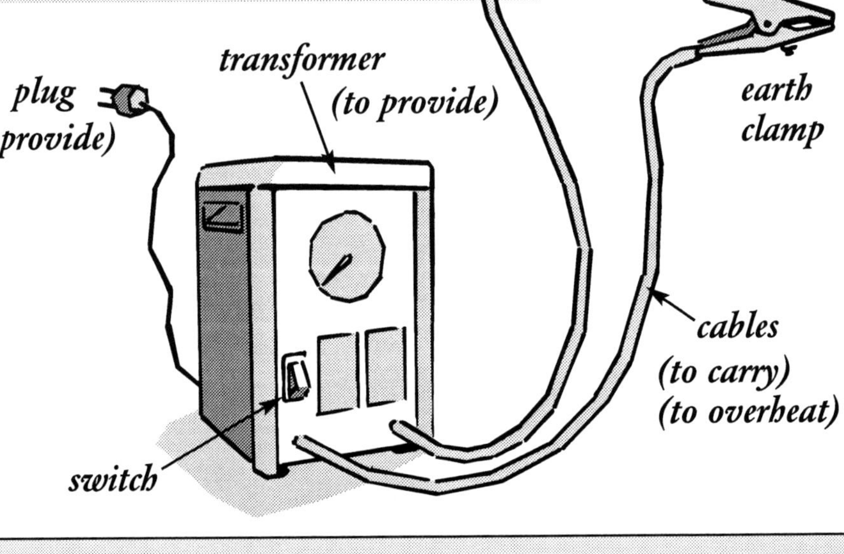

Methods of welding

Lesson **3.5.2**

Gas welding

1. In gas welding it is necessary to use a mixture of two gases. To create a hot enough flame, a combustible gas must be mixed with oxygen. Although acetylene is normally used, the combustible gas need not be acetylene. Hydrogen or petroleum gases can also be used.

2. Oxygen can be stored at very high pressure (120 atmospheres). It is dangerous to compress gaseous acetylene in the same way and so it is dissolved under pressure in liquid acetone but at a much lower pressure than oxygen.

3. To create a suitable flame, the gases must be supplied to the welding torch at low pressure. Pressure regulators are therefore used to regulate the gas flow from the cylinders. They are screwed into the top of each cylinder.

4. Gas welding is normally used to join steel to steel. To make a very strong joint the workpieces must be composed of the same metal. Welding rods are used to provide filler metal. In gas welding these rods are generally made of steel. Bronze or brass rods can also be used.

Find the differences!

Gas welding	Arc welding
1. How are the workpieces melted?	
by a flame that is weated in burning acetylene mixed with oxygen	*by an electric arc that is produced with powerful electric current*
2. What kind of energy is used?	
oxygen, stored at high pressure *acetylene, dissolved in liquid*	*low voltage current*
3. How can you adjust the level of energy?	
pressure regulators control the gas flow	*a current regulator controls/adjusts the number of amperes*
4. What are the names for the joining tools?	
welding torch *welding rod*	*electrode holder* *electrode* *earth clamp*

Arc welding

1. In arc welding the workpieces are not melted by a flame. They are melted by an electric arc. To create the arc a powerful electric current must be provided. The current must at least be 60A or else the current will not create enough heat. For thicker workpieces, the current can be 250A or more. (An electric bulb for example operates at a minimum of 1A).

2. In order to carry this current, the cables from the transformer must be quite thick or else they will overheat. To protect the operator, the electrode holder and the cables must be well-insulated. The welding current must be provided at a low voltage to prevent the danger of electrocution.

3. A transformer is used to supply the necessary current. An earth clamp must be used to complete the electric circuit. The earth clamp must be attached to the workpiece or else the current cannot flow around the circuit and the arc will not appear. It must be securely attached or else an arc will appear between the clamp and the workpiece.

Welding – Safety instructions 1 Lesson **3.6.1**

Gas welding

Zuerst Begriffe anhand der Zeichnungen klären, dann Lückentext bearbeiten.)

1. You must wear ...*goggles*... to protect your eyes.
2. Gas cylinders must be used in ...*upright*... position.
3. Your ...*welding gloves*... should not be oily or greasy. Oxygen can combine with oil or grease to cause an ...*explosion*... .
4. You should wear long ...*sleeves*... so that you cannot burn your arms.
5. You should wear ...*rubber*... ...*boots*... so that you will not burn your feet.
6. You should wear ...*gloves*... so that the ...*sparks*... will not burn your hands.
7. Allow the sparks to fall into a metal container so that they ...*can't*... ...*burn*... the floor.
8. There must be fire extinguishers in the workshop so that any fires can be extinguished immediately.
9. After welding turn ...*off*... all valves so that no gases can ...*escape*... .

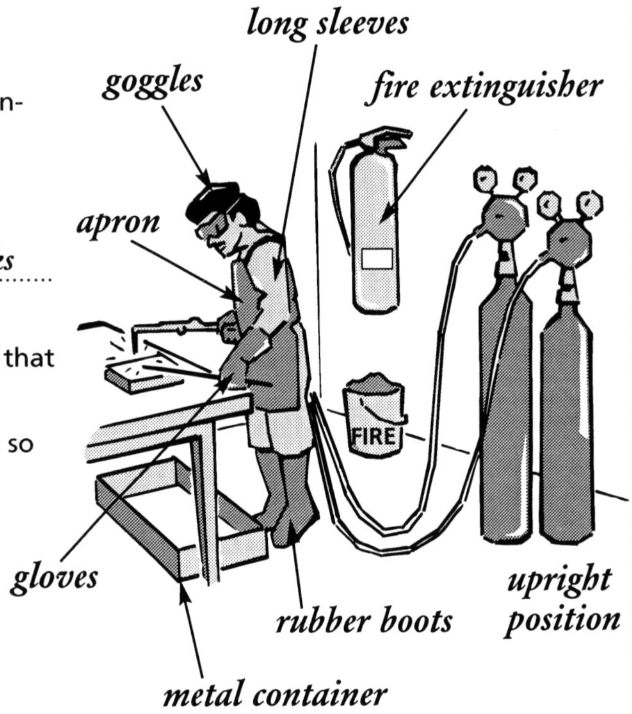

Arc welding

1. A face mask must be used or your eyes will not be ...*protected*... .
2. The workshop floor should be ...*dry*... and ...*clean*... so that it cannot ...*conduct*... electricity.
3. The floor should be made of ...*concrete*... so that it cannot be burnt.
4. Overalls with long ...*sleeves*... should be worn.
5. Thick shoes should be worn to ...*protect*... your feet.
6. Welding gloves should be worn so that your hands are protected from ...*sparks*... .
7. Allow the sparks to fall into a ...*metal container*... so that they don't burn the floor.
8. Fire extinguishers should be in the workshop so that electrical fires can be ...*extinguished*... .
9. After welding all ...*transformers*... must be turned off to prevent accidents.

Welding – Safety instructions 2 Lesson 3.6.2

must / should / must not / should not / could / could not

1. Why must you wear a mask?
   Because you could get a spark in your eyes.
2. Why must you keep your clothes dry?
   Because oxygen in combination with oil or grease could cause an explosion.
3. Why do you wear rubber boots?
   Because you should not burn your feet.
4. Why do you wear an apron and a cap?
   Because your body or hair must not catch fire.
5. Why must the floor be made of concrete?
   Because wooden floors could start burning.
6. Why do you need a metal container?
   Because you must catch all sparks in an inflammable place.

Please help this poor man in the workshop. Give instructions:

1. *Wear long sleeves when welding.*
2. *You must put on rubber boots.*
3. *Welding gloves should be worn.*
4. *Don't look into the ark. Wear a mask.*
5. *Dry the workshop floor. Water is a good conductor.*
6. *Please, turn off the tap completely.*
7. *Make sure you have the right extinguisher.*
8. *Never use a wooden box, it could burn.*

Attack the earth clamp.

Switch the transformer on.

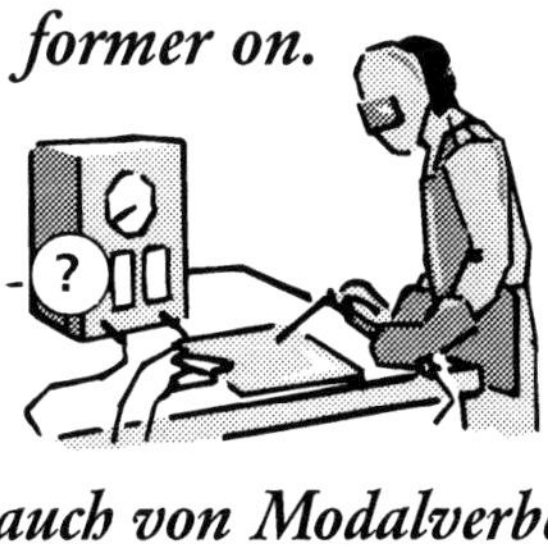

Put the plug in.

Don't move too fast.

(Gebrauch von Modalverben ebenso möglich.)

Soft and hard soldering 1 Lesson 3.7.1

Soft soldering

1. Soldering is a common way of joining metals. All solders are alloys, i.e. mixtures of one or two metals. Soft solder is an alloy of tin and lead.

2. All soldering processes require heat. In soft soldering the heat comes from a soldering iron.

3. The name "iron" is misleading because the tip of the iron is copper. This metal is a good conductor of heat.

4. All metals discolour when they are heated. This is caused by oxidation.

5. Fluxes help the solder to flow and act as a barrier to oxidation. Active fluxes actually dissolve oxides. An active flux for soft soldering is zinc, chloride solution.

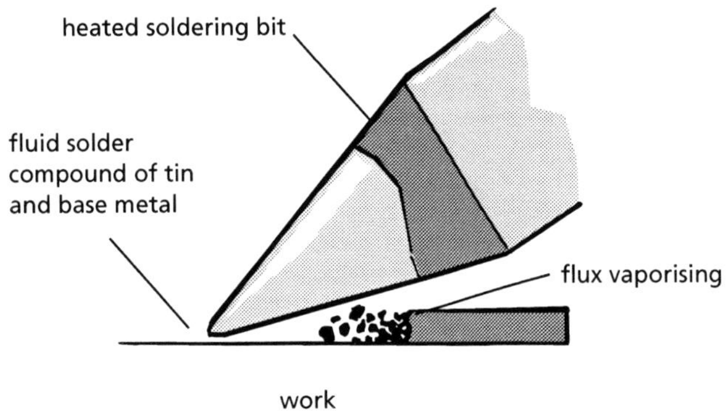

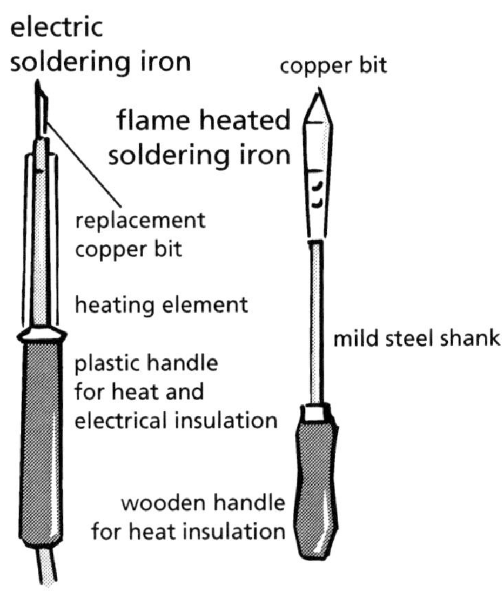

Hard soldering

1. Hard soldering gives a much stronger joint than soft soldering. The solders are harder and the melting temperatures are higher.

2. There are two kinds of hard soldering: brazing, using a copper and zinc alloy as a solder, and silver soldering, using a silver, copper, zinc alloy.

3. In both methods a gas-burning brazing torch is used. The addition of blown air from a compressor produces a very hot flame.

4. The flux for hard soldering is mainly calcinated borax used as powder or mixed into a paste with water.

5. At all soldering the joint must be clean before works begins. Joints consist of metals of different thickness. They must be heated so that the whole joint is brought to the soldering temperature at the same moment.

Soft and hard soldering 2

Lesson **3.7.2**

1. What is soldering?
   Soldering is a common way of joining metals.
2. In what way differs hard soldering from soft soldering?
   The joints are stronger, temperatures higher.
3. What happens when you heat metal?
   The metal discolours because of oxidation.
4. Why are fluxes used?
   Fluxes are needed to reduce oxidation.
5. What is the function of "active fluxes"?
   Active fluxes dissolve oxides.
6. What are the main parts of a soldering iron?
   Wooden handle, heating element, copper bit.
7. Name the two kinds of hard soldering.
   Brazing and silver soldering.
8. What do the fluxes for hard and soft soldering contain?
   Either calcinated borax or zinc cloride solution.
9. What are the working conditions for soldering?
   All joints must be very clean.
10. What are the joints generally made of?
    Normally the joints are made of metals of different thickness.

Antworten auf Seite 71

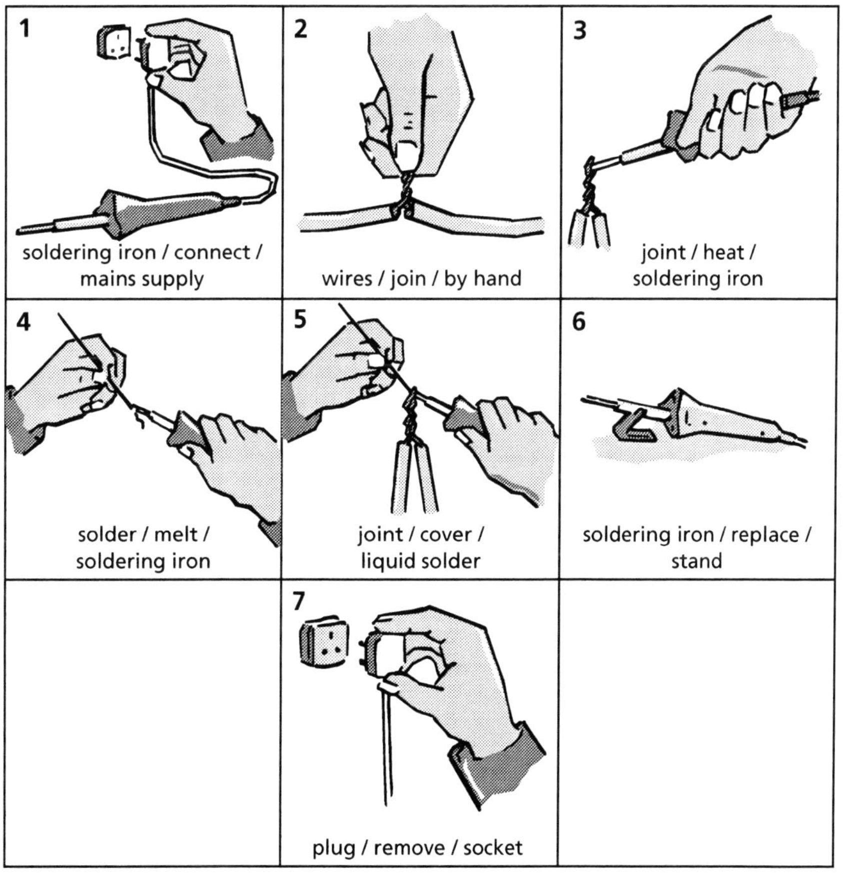

Option 1

How to... – put up a shelve

Lesson **3.7.**

1. Draw a horizontal straight line on the wall.
2. Place the shelf on the line.
3. Place brackets under the shelf.
4. Mark holes on the wall and on the shelf.
5. Make holes in the wall and in the shelf. Use a drill.
6. Insert plugs in the hole in the wall.
7. Screw the brackets to the wall.
8. Caution. Do not overtighten the screws.
9. Place the shelf on the brackets.
10. Move the shelf from side to side, until the holes in the brackets are under the shelf.
11. Screw the shelf on to the brackets.
12. Check that the shelf is tight.

Today's urgency

1. What are these objects called?

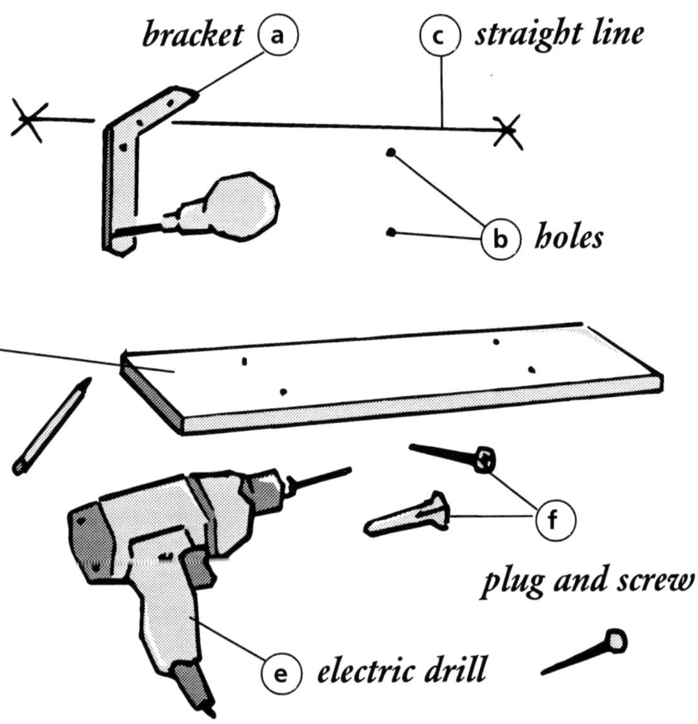

2. Right or wrong? Correct the wrong ones.

	Right	Wrong
2.1. Draw a straight line on the wall. Make sure that it is horizontal.	X	
2.2. Put plugs into the holes in the wall.	X	
2.3. Do not tighten the screws in the wall.		X
2.4. Move the shelf until the holes in the shelf are over the holes in the bracket.	X	

Option 2

How to... – drill a hole in a steel plate

Lesson **3.7.**

A.

NOTE: Before you touch the drilling machine, check that the power is off.

First, you insert the key in the chuck. Then you rotate the key clockwise until the jaws are open. Next, you insert the bit between the jaws. Finally, you rotate the key anticlockwise until the jaws are closed. Before you use the drill, make sure that the bit is tight.

1. Mark the hole on the plate.
2. Put the plate into a vice on the table.
3. Move the table and the vice until the bit is over the mark.
4. Tighten the table and the vice.
5. Switch on the power.
6. Lower the bit and drill the hole carefully.

1. What are the objects in the diagram called?

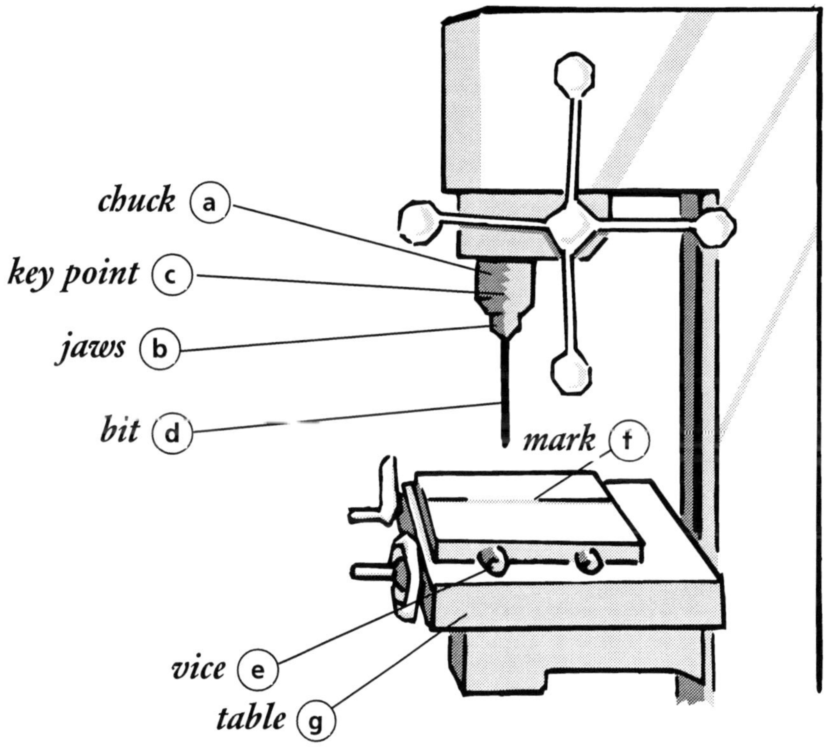

2. Answer these questions:

2.1. How do you open the jaws? *You turn the key anti-clockwise.*

2.2. How do you close the jaws? *You turn the key clockwise.*

3. Right or wrong? Correct the wrong ones.

	Right	Wrong
3.1. Make sure that the power is off. Then put the key into the chuck.	X	
3.2. You use the drill before you check that the bit is tight.		X
3.3. Move the table and vice until the mark is under the bit.	X	
3.4. Tighten the table using the vice.		X

1. Name at least 10 parts.

2. Answer the following questions.

2.1. What kind of clothes do you have to wear if you weld workpieces?

You must wear long sleeves, rubber boots, welding gloves and a mask.

2.2. What do you need to mix oxygen and acetylene?

You need an oxygen cylinder, pressure and a torch.

2.3. How do you regulate the gas consumption?

You can regulate the gas flow with the valve.

2.4. Why do some metals discolour when they are heated?

Because they oxydate.

2.5. What material does the tip of the soldering iron consist of ?

It consists of copper.

2.6. What metals can be used as solder?

tin, zinc, and alloys

3. Join the right parts of the sentences.

1.	In gas welding it is necessary	*E*	A.	to regulate the gas flow.
2.	To create a suitable flame	*G*	B.	the workpieces must be composed of the same metal.
3.	Pressure regulators are used	*A*	C.	to protect the operator.
4.	Gas welding is normally used	*F*	D.	is an alloy of tin and lead.
5.	To make a very strong joint	*B*	E.	to use a mixture of two gases.
6.	To create an electric arc	*J*	F.	to join steel to steel.
7.	The electrode holder and the cables must be well-insulated	*C*	G.	the gases must be supplied at low pressure.
8.	Soft solder	*D*	H.	and act as a barrier to oxidation.
9.	Fluxes help the solder to flow	*H*	I.	to complete the electric circuit.
10.	An earth clamp must be used	*I*	J.	a powerful electric current must be provided.

4. True or false?

	True	No
After welding you needn´t turn off all valves.		X
You should wear Doc Marten´s* to protect your feet.	X	
Fluxes help the solder to flow between the workpieces.	X	
All metals don´t discolour when heated.		X
The floor should be made of wood so that it can´t be burnt.		X
You can use a welding torch for soldering.		X

* bekannte englische Schuhfirma

5. Translate into English.

5.1. Ein Schutzschild muss benutzt werden, um die Augen zu schützen.
A face mask must be used to protect the eyes.

5.2. Feuerlöscher müssen in jeder Werkstatt sein.
Fire extinguishers must exist in every workshop.

5.3. Schweißen wird zum Verbinden von Stahlteilen benutzt.
Welding is used to join pieces of steel.

5.4. Das Ventil regelt den Gasfluss.
The valve regulates the gas flow.

5.5. Zum Weichlöten benötigt man einen Lötkolben.
For soft soldering you need a soldering iron.

5.6. Flußmittel unterstützen den Lötvorgang.
Fluxes support the soldering process.

5.7. Hartlöten schafft eine festere Verbindung und die Schmelztemperaturen sind höher.
Hard soldering gives a much stronger joint and the melting temperatures are higher.

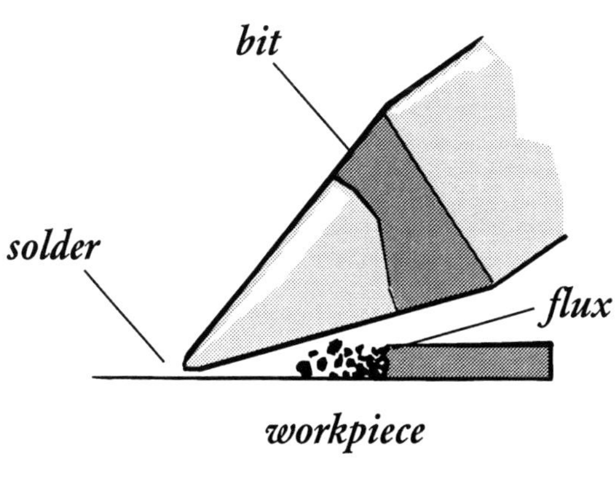

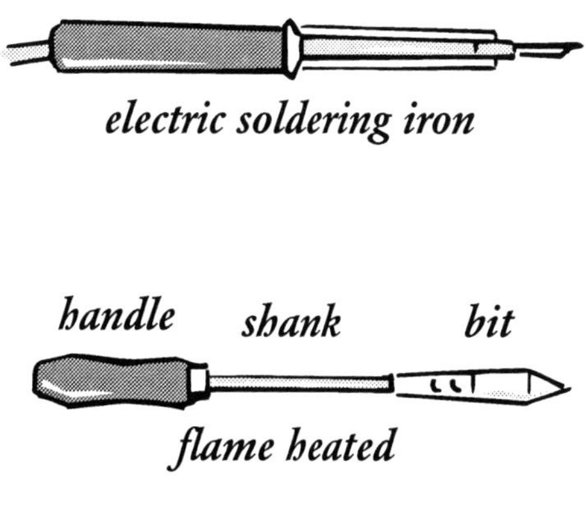

Vocab-check – Welding and soldering

Lesson **3.8.3**

1	accident	*Unfall*
2	acetylene	*Acetylen*
3	alloy	*Legierung*
4	appropriate	*zugehörig*
5	apron	*Schürze*
6	arc	*Lichtbogen*
7	barrier	*Barriere*
8	brass	*Messing*
9	bronze	*Bronze*
10	combustible	*brennbar*
11	concrete	*Beton*
12	conductor	*Leiter (elektr.)*
13	copper	*Kupfer*
14	current	*Strom*
15	earth clamp	*Erdklammer*
16	electrocution	*Elektroschock*
17	electrode holder	*Elektrodenhalter*
18	face mask	*Maske*
19	filler metal	*Füllmetall*
20	fire extinguisher	*Feuerlöscher*
21	flux	*Flussmittel*
22	gas cylinder	*Gasflasche*
23	gas flow	*Gasfluss*
24	goggles	*Schutzbrille*
25	grease	*Schmiermittel*
26	hose	*Schlauch*
27	hydrogen	*Wasserstoff*
28	lead	*Blei*
29	liquid solder	*flüssiges Lötmetall*
30	joint	*Verbindung*
31	oxygen	*Sauerstoff*
32	powerful	*kräftig*
33	pressure gauge	*Druckanzeiger*
34	pressure regulator	*Druckregulator*
35	solder	*Lötmetall*
36	soldering	*Löten*
37	spark	*Funke*
38	thickness	*Dicke*
39	tin	*Zinn/Blech*
40	tip	*Spitze*
41	to adjust	*einstellen*
42	to be composed of	*bestehen aus*
43	to be provided	*zur Verfügung stellen*
44	to be stored	*gelagert werden*
45	to be supplied	*versorgt werden*
46	to compress	*verdichten*
47	to discolour	*verfärben*
48	to dissolve	*sich auflösen*
49	to fuse	*verschmelzen*
50	to insulate	*isolieren*
51	to melt	*schmelzen*
52	to overheat	*überhitzen*
53	to prevent	*vorbeugen*
54	to provide	*beschaffen*
55	to vaporise	*verflüchtigen*
56	to weld	*schweißen*
57	valve	*Ventil*
58	welding gloves	*Schweißhandschuhe*
59	welding rod	*Schweißstab*
60	welding torch	*Schweißbrenner*
61	well-insulated	*gut isoliert*
62	workpiece	*Werkstück*
63		
64		
65		
66		
67		
68		
69		
70		

1. Try to identify the correct tools with the help of these words:

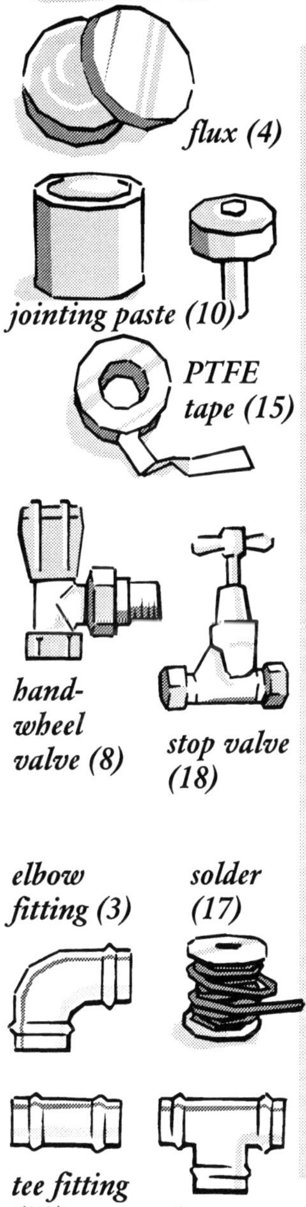

English	German
1. bath wrench	*Badewannenschlüssel*
2. bleeding of radiator	*entlüften*
3. elbow fitting	*Ellbogengelenk*
4. flux	*Flussmittel*
5. gas blowlamp	*Lötlampe*
6. gate valve	*Absperrhahn*
7. hand bender	*(Biegewerkzeug)*
8. handwheel valve	*Eckventil*
9. hole saw	*Lochsäge*
10. jointing paste	*Dichtpaste*
11. pillar tap	*Standarmatur*
12. pipe clips	*Rohrschellen*
13. pipe cutter	*Rohrschneider*
14. pipe wrench	*Rohrzange*
15. PTFE tape	*Isolierband*
16. sink mixer	*Mischbatterie*
17. solder	*Lötzinn, Weichlot*
18. stop valve	*Absperrventil*
19. tank cutter	*Lochschneider*
20. tee fitting	*Rohrverbindung T-Stück*
21. thermostatic valve	*Thermostatventil*
22. trap	*Geruchsverschluss, Siphon*
23. washers	*Unterlegscheibe*
24. wire wool	*Drahtwolle*

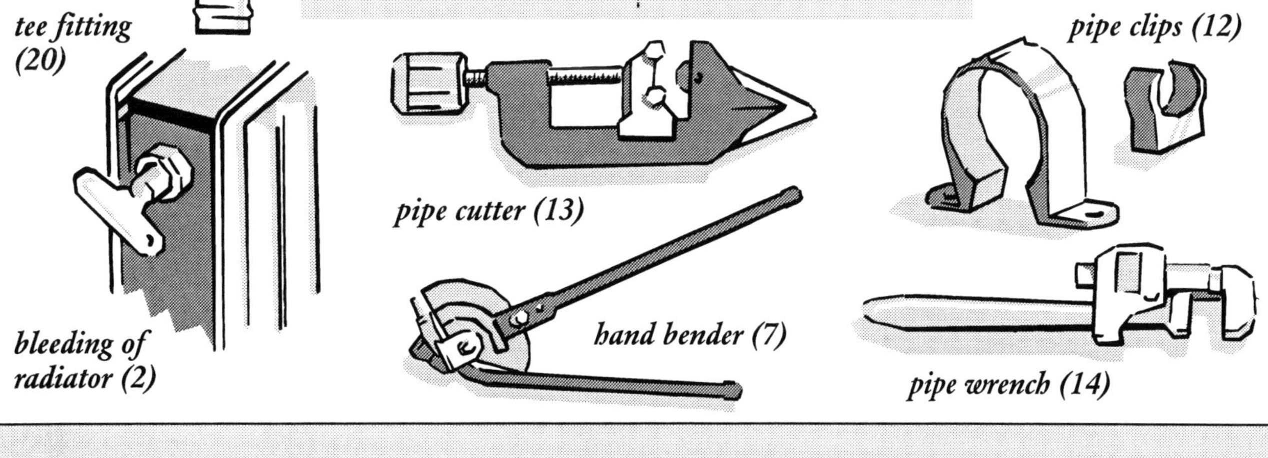

2. Name the correct tools or materials.
Then underline all verbs. How many different verbs can you find? ***(siehe Seite 71)***

Bitte Arbeitsanweisungen Seite 72 beachten.

A	B	C	
A tool that is needed to reach tap connectors under the bath. *bath wrench (1)*	Used for cleaning the pipe ends before soldering. *wire wool (24)*	Many models are available. With a replaceable cartridge it provides an easy controllable hot flame, ideal for plumbing. *gas blowlamp (5)*	1
Open the vent at the top of the radiator until you hear gurgling sounds. With a cloth held ready, close the vent with the key when water starts to spray out. *bleeding of radiator (2)*		A metal gate operates inside the body and there is no replaceable washer, so it is often used to isolate hot water cylinders and feed expansion tanks. *gate valve (6) – (ohne Abb.)*	2
Used on copper pipes and fittings before soldering. It helps the solder to run freely. *flux (4)*	A very thin and comfortable plastic tape which is put around the threads of fittings. *PTFE tape (15)*	This tool bends all sizes of copper pipe without problems. *hand bender (7)*	3
Used on compression joints to make a watertight seal. *jointing paste (10)*	Plumbers used this a lot for all soldering processes. *solder (17)*	For quick and easy cutting of various sized holes in tanks etc. *hole saw (9)*	4
This is the standard tap you find in all households, usually chrome-plated or brass. *pillar tap (11)*	Used to join three ends of a copper pipe. *tee fittings (20)*	A hacksaw can easily cut copper pipe, but this tool cuts an accurate square end easily and quickly. The pointed end removes burrs from the end of the pipes. *pipe cutter (13)*	5
Various models of this mixer are available with long swinging arms to deliver the water over a basin or a double sink. *sink mixer (16)*	A useful tool for undoing large pipe nuts. *pipe wrench (14) also called stillsons*	Often used to control the whole house water supply. When fitting make sure that the arrow at the side is matching the actual water flow. *stop valve (18)*	6
Used in a carpenter's brace, this tool cuts holes from 25 mm to 125 mm in plastic water tanks. *tank cutter (19) – (ohne Abbildung)*		This device senses the temperature around in the room closes it off and opens it again when the temperature is falling. Very useful in kitchens and all other rooms. *thermostatic valve (21)*	7
The purpose is to seal the installation from foul air rising from the drain. This is achieved by a reservoir of water which is collected in the bend. *trap (22)*	These are put between the links of two pipes to ensure a watertight and secure joint. *washers (23)*	These can be used at regular intervals on both horizontal and vertical pipe runs. Types are available for copper and plastic types. *tee fittings (20)*	8

Plumbing – Everything spick-and-span

Lesson **3.10.1**

This is the Rick's bathroom in his new apartment. Everything is new. His landlord is very proud of it, but Rick has to pay a lot of rent.

1. Try to spot these items:

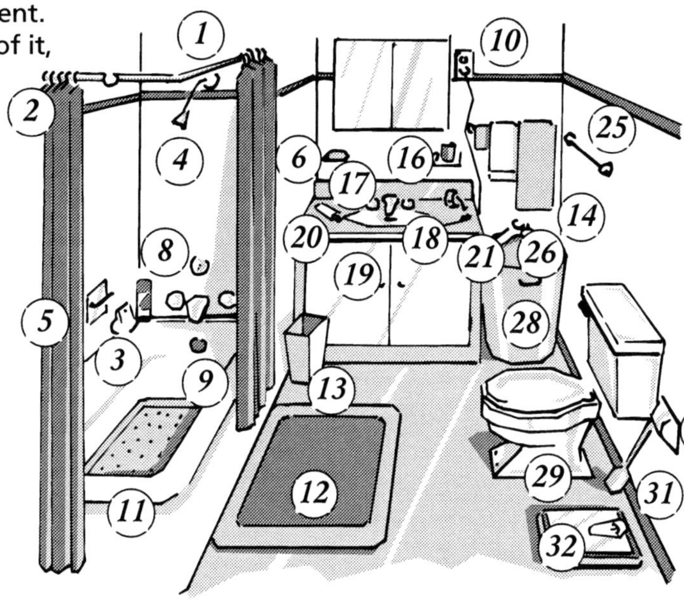

1. curtain rail	9. drain	17. hot water tap	25. towel rack
2. curtain rings	10. plug	18. cold water tap	26. hair dryer
3. shower cap	11. bath tub	19. sink	27. tiles
4. shower head	12. mat	20. nailbrush	28. basket
5. shower curtain	13. rubbish bin	21. toothbrush	29. toilet
6. soap dish	14. medicine chest	22. wash cloth	30. toilet paper
7. sponge	15. soap	23. towel	31. toilet brush
8. Head and Shoulders	16. tooth paste	24. bath towel	32. scales

Five years later Rick wants to move in with his new girl-friend Ellis. Her apartment is much bigger and she pays less rent. He also likes the idea of having somebody permantly around him who does all the cooking, cleaning, shopping and so on ...

This is what his bathroom looks like today

2. Explain what is wrong.
Use the given adjectives below.

English	German
1. tarnished	*angelaufen, fleckig*
2. filthy, dirty	*schmutzig*
3. twisted	*verbogen*
4. dented	*verbeult*
5. scratched	*verkratzt*
6. cracked	*gesprungen*
7. peeled	*abgeblättert*
8. used	*verbraucht*
9. clogged up	*verstopft*
10. blocked	*blockiert*
11. rusty	*verrostet*
12. worn	*abgenutzt*
13. stained	*befleckt*
14. muddy	*verdreckt, nass*
15. obstructed	*versperrt*
16. bent	*verbogen*
17.	
18.	
19.	

Plumbing – Everything spick-and-span — Lesson **3.10.2**

When Ellis sees this mess she tells Rick what to do because the landlord is not willing to accept the desaster.

3. Complete statements and instructions.

1. The cold water tap is stained.	**Wipe the stains off.**
2. The shower curtain is *used.*	*Buy a new one.*
3. The shower head is *blocked.*	*Clean it carefully.*
4. The soap dish is *dented.*	*Replace it.*
5. The medicine chest is *dirty.*	*Empty it completely and then clean it.*

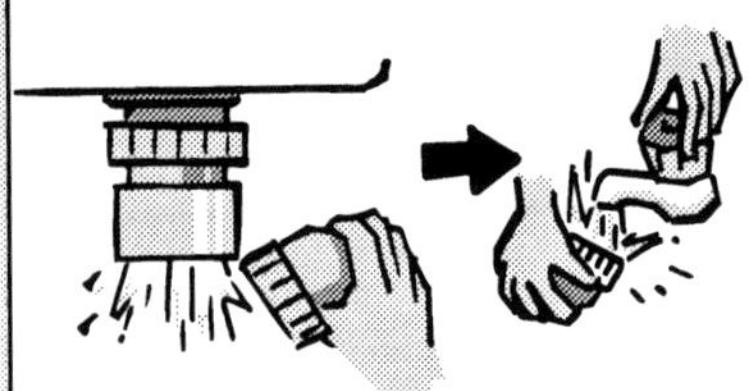

6. The tiles are *scratched.*	*Call a tiler to replace them.*
7. The paint has *peeled.*	*Decorate the bathroom.*
8. The bath tub is *filthy.*	*Don't scratch it.* *Clean it carefully.*
9. The hot water tap is *tarnished.*	
10. The drain *is clogged up.*	*Ask a plumber to clear it.*

11. The sink *is obstructed.*	*Open the trap and clean it.*
12. The curtain rings *are twisted.*	*Buy new ones.*
13. The scales are out of order.	*Ask a mechanic to fix them.*
14. The bath mat *is stained.*	*Put it into the washing machine.*
15. The pipes *are rusty.*	*Exchange them with new ones.*

After the landlord has had a look, he is not satisfied with the condition of the bathroom. He tells Rick what it should be like.

4. Translate: ***(siehe Seite 72)***

1. Der Wasserhahn sollte glänzen.
2. Der Duschvorhang sollte sauber sein.
3. Das Wasser sollte aus dem Brausekopf fließen.
4. Man sollte die Seife ablegen können.
5. Man sollte sich im Spiegel sehen können.
6. Die Fliesen sollten ersetzt werden.
7. Die Wandfarbe sollte erneuert werden.
8. Man sollte immer sorgfältig sein.
9. Der Wasserhahn sollte leicht zu drehen sein.
10. Das Bad sollte nicht übel riechen.
11. Man sollte nichts liegen lassen.
12. Man sollte nur Flüssigkeiten in den Abfluß schütten.
13. Man sollte eine neue Badematte kaufen.
14. Man sollte die Rohre reinigen.
15. Alles sollte wie neu aussehen.

Thinking about all this work Rick decided not to move in with his girl-friend but stay a bachelor instead.

Toolbox 4 – Building and plastering

1. Try to identify the correct tools with the help of these words:

English	German
1. bolster chisel	*Putzmeißel*
2. bricklayer´s trowel	*Maurerspachtel*
3. builder´s level	*Wasserwaage*
4. builder´s square	*Anlegewinkel*
5. claw hammer	*Zimmermannshammer*
6. club hammer	*Fäustel*
7. concrete mixer	*Betonmischmaschine*
8. corner trowels	*Winkelspachtel*
9. earth rammer	*Erdstampfer*
10. hawk	*Mörtelbrett*
11. line and pins	*Richtschnur*
12. mixing shovel	*Schaufel*
13. nail punches	*Körner*
14. plasterer´s trowl	*Putzkelle*
15. plugging chisel	*Stechbeitel*
16. scratcher	*Kratzer*
17. stiff broom	*Besen*
18. track lifter	*Fugenzieher*
19. wheelbarrow	*Schubkarre*
20. wooden float	*Holzkelle*
21. pin hammer	*Zapfenhammer*

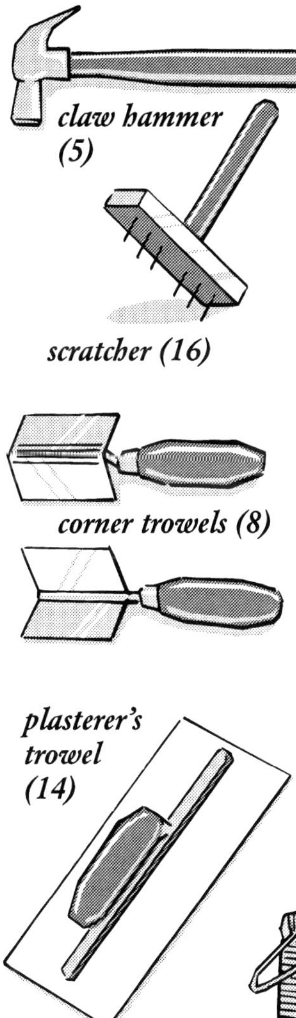

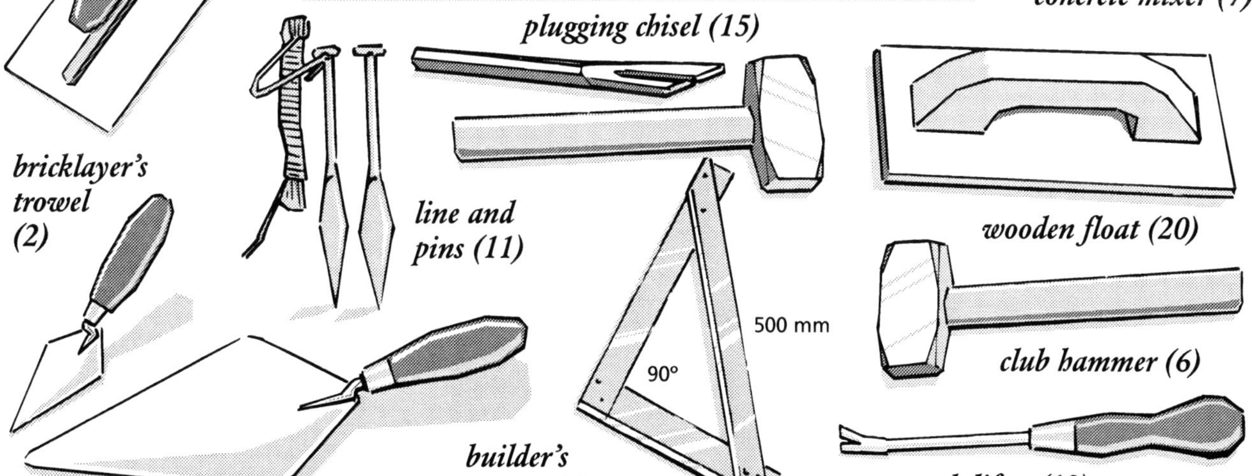

2. Name the correct tools.
Bitte Arbeitsanweisungen Seite 72 beachten.

A	B	C	
The claw is used to lever out the nail when it has been knocked back from the other side of the timber. *claw hammer (5)*	Ideally a square mouth shovel with turned up edges. A garden spade is not very useful. *mixing shovel (12)*	For levering out tacks, small nails and pins. *track lifter (18)*	**1**
Use this to firm the soil and hardcore. This is very important for the sub-base. *earth rammer (9)*		Essential for the all-important cleaning up. *stiff broom (17)*	**2**
Good one have a spring blade riveted to an aluminium alloy frame and a hardwood handle. *plasterer's trowels (14)*	For punching nail heads below the surface. Many sizes are available. *nail punch (13)*	Use this one to finish the undercoat. It gives it a grainy texture and provides a good surface for the topcoat. *wooden float (20)*	**3**
Used for finishing the angles of walls which is always difficult. *corner trowels (8)*		You will use this a lot to check the horizontal and vertical placing of bricks. *builder's level (3)* *builder's square (4)*	**4**
These give you a quick and easy guide when laying a line of bricks. *line and pins (11)*		This special chisel fits between the bricks and can remove old mortar neatly. *plugging chisel (15)*	**5**
These will be necessary if you are removing old plaster from the walls. Best to wear goggles while using these tools. *bolster chisel (1)* *club hammer (6)*		These tools have one straight and one curved edge to the blade and are either left or right-handed. Used for applying concrete. *bricklayer's travel (2)*	**6**
This tool is used to transport mixed concrete or other materials that you need to transport. *wheelbarrow (19)*	Something else you can make yourself from six nails knocked into a timber wood and with their heads cut off. It is used to scratch the surface of the partly dried undercoat to provide a good key for the finishing. *scratcher (16)*	A very useful too to check 90 degree angle. For setting out corners this is absolutely necessary. *builder's square (3)*	**7**

Welche Bestandteile hat Zement?

(Translation exercise)

1. Zement wird normalerweise aus Kalkstein und Ton hergestellt, jedoch werden ebenso Kreide und Sand verwendet. Diese Materialien werden in eine große Maschine gefüllt, die diese in kleine Stücke zermahlt und vermischt. Diese Mischung wird dann in einem Brennofen erhitzt. Nach dem Abkühlen wird sie zu feinem Zementpuder zermahlen.
2. Das wichtigste Mineral in Zement ist Kalk, der hauptsächlich aus Kalkstein gewonnen wird, ebenso Kieselerde und Tonerde, die durch Ton zur Verfügung gestellt werden. Manchmal wird auch Eisen verwendet.
3. Nach dem Zermahlen und Mischen werden die verschiedenen Zutaten in einem sich drehenden Brennofen gegeben und auf 1500 Grad Celsius erhitzt.
4. Dieses Erhitzen produziert Schlacke, die dann mit einem Mineral, genannt Gips, zu einem Puder vermahlen wird. Dieses wird hinzugefügt um die Zeit des Erhärtens des Zements zu regulieren.
5. Wenn man Wasser zum Zementpuder hinzufügt, verbinden sich die beiden Grundstoffe und produzieren eine feste Verbindung, wenn der Zement hart wird.

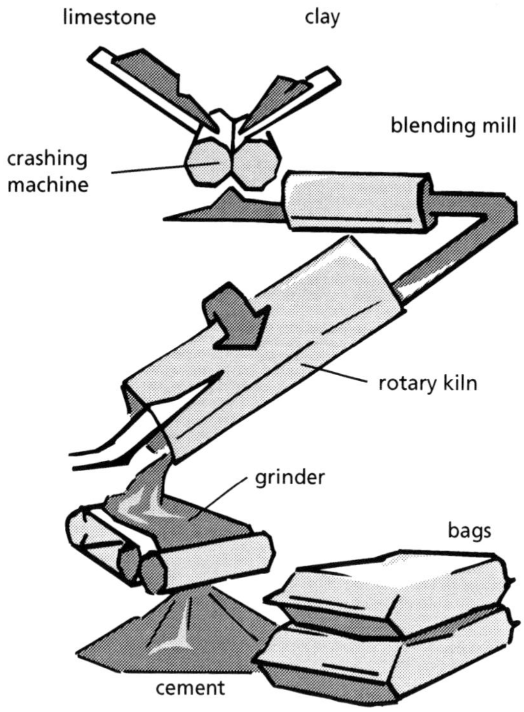

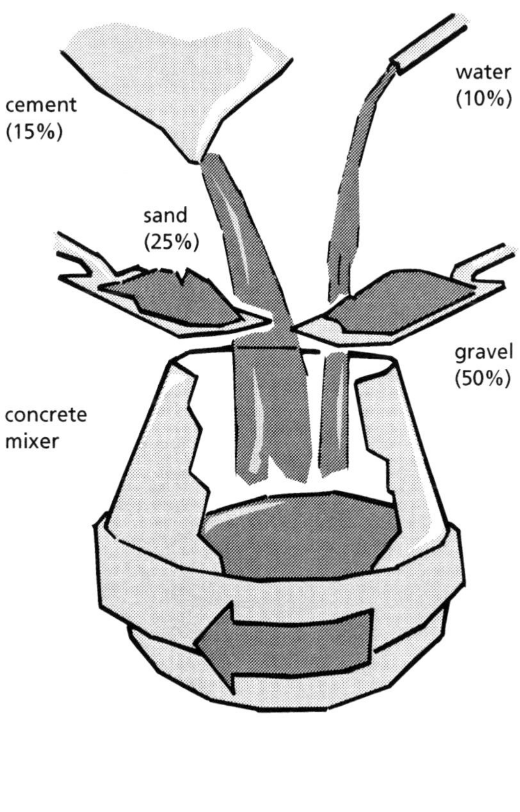

Wie macht man Beton?

1. Beton wird hergestellt, wenn man Kieselsteine oder kleine Steine zusammen mit Sand und Zement mischt.
2. Diese Materialien werden in einem sich drehenden Mischer gelegt oder mit einem Spaten vermischt.
3. Beton ist eine Breimasse, die sich verfestigt und ein hartes Material erzeugt. Es wird als Baustoff bei der Errichtung von Wänden, Fußböden, Straßen, Brücken und Dämmen verwendet.
4. Der meiste Beton wird in einer Mischmaschine hergestellt, die sich dreht und die Zutaten immer wieder in Bewegung hält, so dass sie sich sehr gut vermischen.
5. Die Mischmaschine wird auf den Kopf gestellt und bis auf den Boden ausgeschüttet. Dann wird der Beton in eine Gussform getragen oder gepumpt, in der er erhärtet und die Form der Gussform annimmt.
6. Beton ist aber nicht sehr fest und muss deshalb verstärkt werden, oftmals indem man Eisenstangen in den Beton mit hineinstellt und ihn so verstärkt.

How to... – prepare a foundation for a brick wall   Lesson 3.12.

1. Mark out the trench with lines and pegs.
2. Dig out the trench with a pickaxe and shovel until it is about 150 mm deep and 300 mm wide.
3. Check that the floor of the trench is horizontal using a plumb-and-level.
5. Place pegs in the floor of the trench and stretch a line between them.
6. Check that the line is horizontal.
7. Fill up the trench evenly with concrete until it is level with the line.
8. Leave the concrete until it is hard.
9. Build the wall on the concrete.

1. What are these things called?

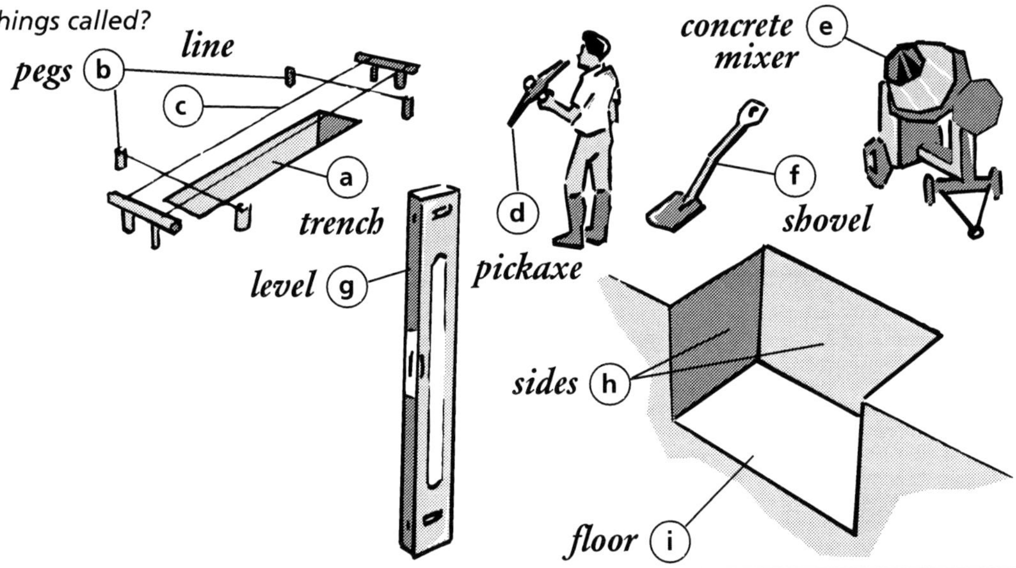

2. Answer these questions

2.1. What is the width of the trench? ***300 mm***

2.2. What is its depth? ***150 mm***

2.3. How do you check that the sides of the trench are vertical? ***By using a plumb.***

2.4. How do you check that the line is horizontal. ***By using a level.***

3. Complete these:

3.1. Between the pegs there is a ***line.***

3.2. Mark out the trench before you ***dig.***

3.3. Check that the concrete is hard before you ***build the wall.***

4. Look at this, then answer the questions:

4.1. What does "plumb" mean? ***vertical***

4.2. What does "level" mean? ***horizontal***

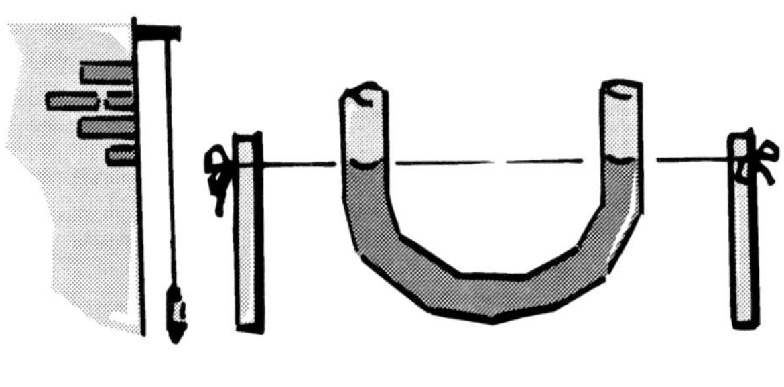

How to... – mix concrete by hand

Lesson **3.12.**

Concrete is made from cement, aggregate and a small amount of water. The aggregate is both coarse (e.g. stones and gravel) and fine (e.g. sand). The coarse aggregate, fine aggregate and the cement are usually in the ration 4:2:1.

1. Put two shovelfuls of sand into a wheelbarrow.
2. Add a shovelful of cement.
3. Mix these thoroughly with a shovel.
4. Add four shovelfuls of gravel.
   Mix thoroughly.
5. Make a hollow in the middle.
   Add a little water with a hose.
   CAUTION:
   Do not add all of the water only a little.
6. Mix the materials thoroughly.
7. Add more water and mix again, until the concrete is the correct thickness.

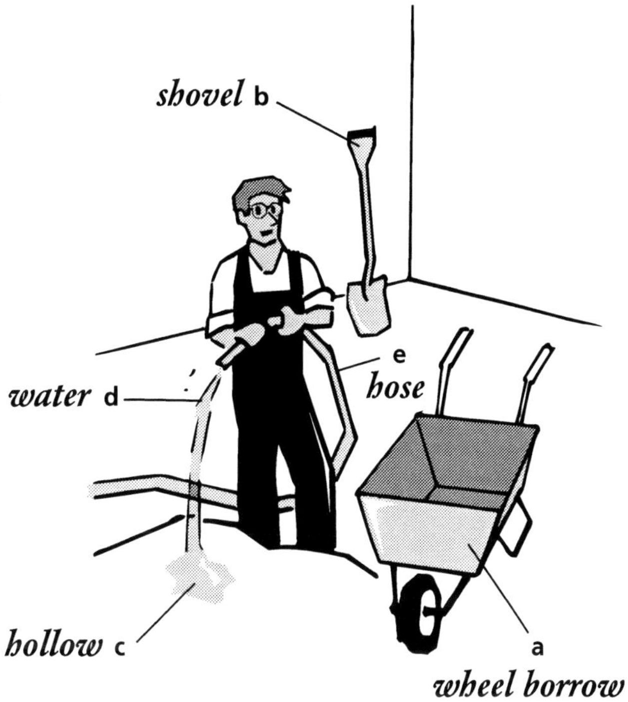

1. What are the correct words for the spaces?

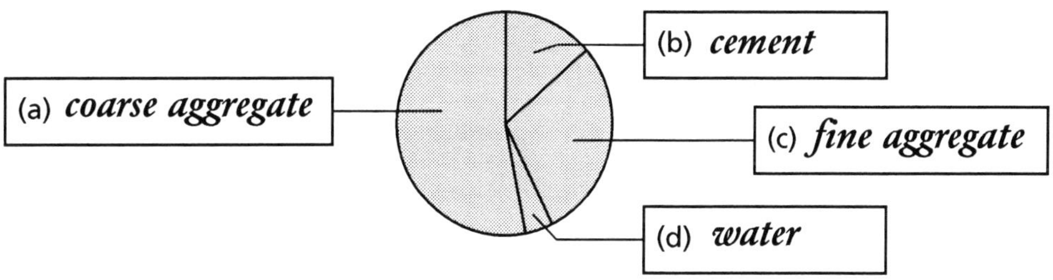

2. Answer these questions

2.1. You want to make 7 cubic metres of concrete. How much aggregate do you need? *6*
2.2. How much cement do you buy? *1 cubic metre*
2.3. How much fine aggregate do you buy? *2 cubic metre*
2.4. How much coarse aggregate do you buy? *4 cubic metre*
2.5. Why do you mix two shovelfuls of sand with one of cement and four of gravel?
Why not one shovelful of each? *Because the ration must be 4 : 2 : 1*

1. *Try to identify the correct tools with the help of these words:*

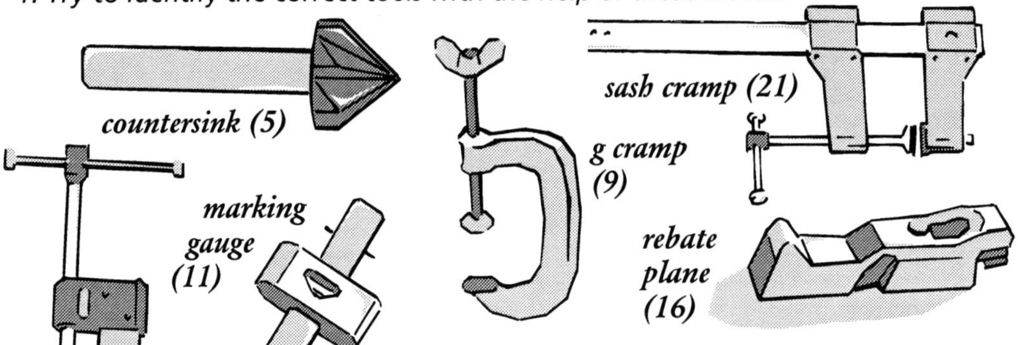

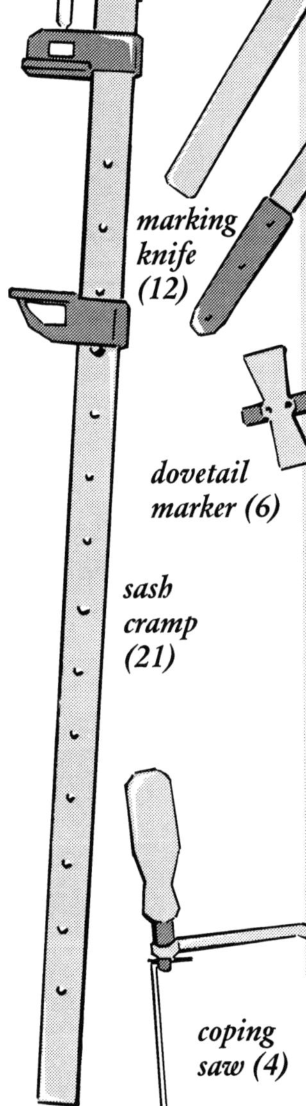

English	German
1. block plane	*Handhobel*
2. bradawl	*Dübelbohrer*
3. chisel	*Stechbeitel*
4. coping saw	*Laubsäge*
5. countersink	*Spitzsenker*
6. dovetail marker	*Schwalbenschwanzmarker*
7. dovetail saw	*Schwalbenschwanzsäge*
8. fret saw	*Laubsäge*
9. g cramp	*Schraubzwinge*
10. hook scraper	*Schaber, Kratzer*
11. marking gauge	*Passlehre*
12. marking knife	*Markiermesser*
13. mitre box	*Gehrlade*
14. mitre cramp	*Gehrungskrampe*
15. mortise gauge	*Zapfenstreichmaß*
16. rebate plane	*Holzhobel*
17. spokeshave	*Schabeisen*
18. surform files	*(Spezialfeile)*
19. try square	*Richtscheit*
20. twist drills	*Spiralbohrer*
21. sash cramp	*Schraubzwinge*

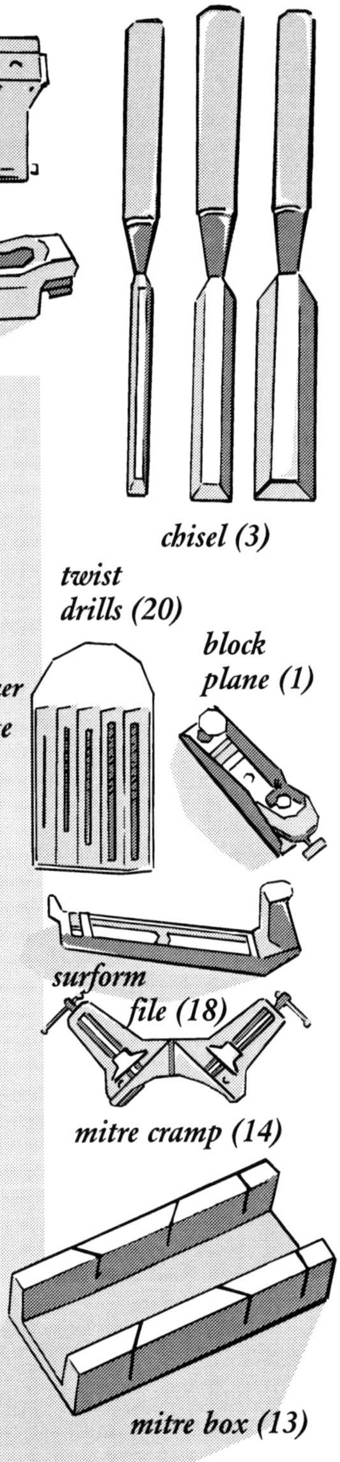

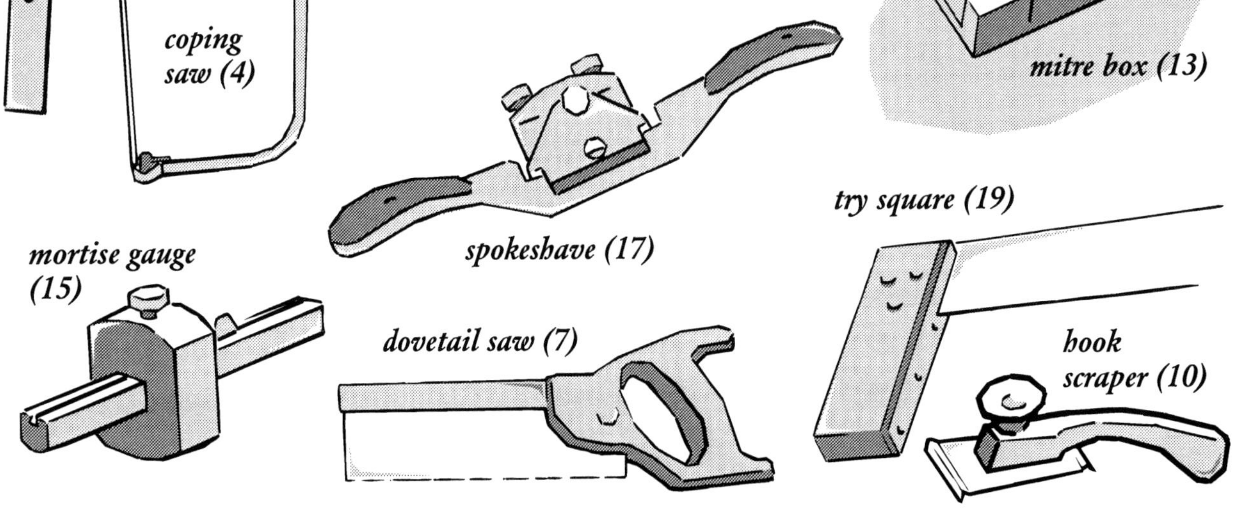

2. Name the correct tools.
Then underline all verbs. How many different verbs can you find?
Bitte Arbeitsanweisungen Seite 72 beachten.

A	B	C	
Best to buy a basic set of three in the following sizes: 6 mm, 19 mm, 38 mm. *chisels (3)*	Used for starting holes before drilling, it can also be used for drilling small screws into softwood. *bradawl – (ohne Abb.)*	Needed to hold wood while you are working on it. Needed when the vice is too small. Best for holding joints while the glue sets. *g cramps (9)*	1
	Needed for sinking screws flush with the surface. *countersink (5)*	Many designs available, some in hardwood, some with metal guides, others in plastic or metal. The help the workers cut the perfect mitre. *mitre box (13)*	2
This tool has two pins which are adjusted to the width of the mortise and which can be marked in one pass and repeated on other workpieces. *mortise gauge (15)*	Made of brass, these are used for marking dovetail saw cuts. The wider side is for softwood and the other for hardwood. *dovetail marker (6)*		3
A moveable jaw slides along the beam to produce positive locking action. *cramp*	This saw is for fine work, because you can move the blade to any direction. *coping saw (4)*	When working very precisely, a scored line can be more accurate than a pencil line. This tool does it. *marking knife (12)*	4
Smaller than the tenon saw, this finely-toothed saw assists in the cutting of accurate joints. *dovetail saw (7)*		This cramp will adjust to the width of most mouldings, which is useful in gluing up picture frames for example. *mitre cramp (14)*	5
A good quality tool of this kind is necessary for making right angles and checking frames after gluing. *try square (19)*	With its blade set at a much lower angle than the smoothing plane, this too is especially designed to cut end grain. *block plane (1)*	For cutting inner shapes in thin material. *fret saw (8)*	6
	A special blade design characterises the surform range. The exchangeable flexible blade has perforations to allow removing the waste very rapidly. *surform files (18)*	This tool is used for marking a line parallel to the edge on a piece of timber, as, for example, before planing down. *marking gauge (11)*	7
This set will serve for both metal and woodworking. *twist drills (20)*	A shaped wooden handle and hook blades make this tool a useful alternative to cabinet scrapers. *hook scraper (10)*	Originally made for wheelwrights. It is very useful for cleaning up curves. *spokeshave (17)*	8

Security around the house

Lesson **3.13.1**

Invitation to burglars. How to enter a house.

The Millers are on holiday and Harry Longfinger pays a visit to their house.
There are possible ways how he could enter the house.
What can we do to keep Harry out?

1. Doors

A rim latch (the sort of lock that allows you to slam the door without a handle on the outside) on the front door and a two lever mortise lock on the back door. These should be replaced by deadlocks (locks which can be locked by a key from both sides and cannot be opened without it). They should make sure that the lock has at least a five-lever mechanism, because two-lever locks are not secure enough for outside doors. The lock must be fitted into the stile (side frame) with key-holes only at the outside and inside of the door. A rim latch is not very safe because it can easily be broken.

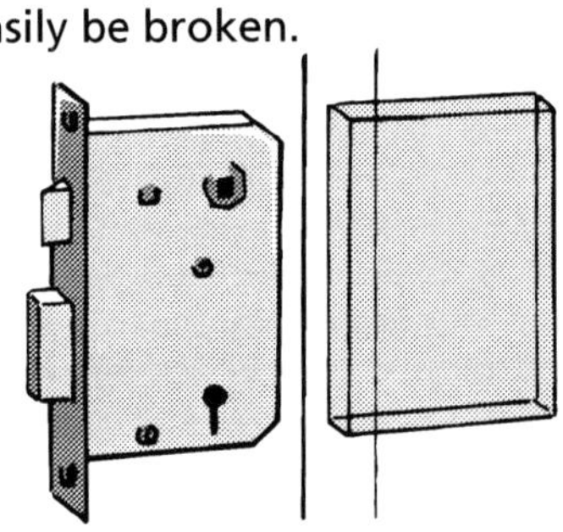

A security chain limits the opening of a door so that you can identify callers. The Millers should have a very strong one which is securely fastened with long srews.

A door viewer at eye level allows a wide angle view of the outside so that you can check the identity and number of callers.

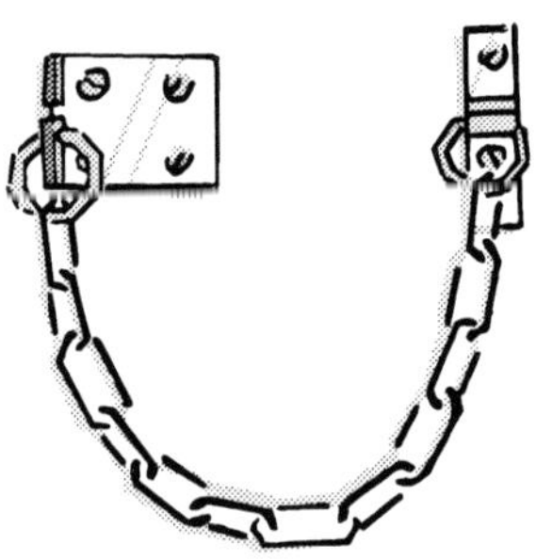

2. Windows

WIndows are the favourite point of entry and if they are locked, the thief must break a pane of glass. Rotten windows are easily levered open, so make sure the frames are sound. The majority of window locks are designed for timber windows, but some locks for metal win-dows are secured by self-tapping screws.

Cockspur handle locks
There are variousy methods of locking the cockspur handle (the small lever on the side of casement windows) including a key operated replacement handle. This one has a pivoting cover, which flips back when unlocked to release the handle.

Mortise door and window bolts
Suitable for timber doors and windows, these neat and unobtrusive locks are fitted into the frame, and a racked bold is wound out with a key.

Security around the house

Lesson **3.13.2**

BEWARE! CAUTION!

Harry Longfinger is at the Miller's door. But the Millers know how to protect their house.

Make sentences by putting the words into the right order!

1. Rim latch / don't / on / the / front door / they / have / a
   They don't have a rim latch on the front door.
2. No / is / two-lever mortise / the back door / there / on
   There is no two-lever mortise on the back door.
3. Only last month / on both doors / were / deadlocks / installed / mechanism / five-lever / which / have / a
   Only last month deadlocks which have a five-lever mechanism were installed on both doors.
4. They / that / not / are / enough / for / know / secure / two-lever locks / outside doors
   They know that two-lever locks are not secure enough for outside doors.
5. Also / are / security chains / there / on both / doors
   There are also security chains on both doors.

Bad luck for Harry! Now he tries the kitchen window.

6. Tries / he / open / lerver / window / to / the / but / sound / the / is / frame
   He tries to open the window lever but the frame is sound.
7. Beside / firmly / is / window / the / locked / a bolt / by
   The window beside is firmly locked by a bolt.
8. Harry / pane / breaks / finally / glass / of / a
   Finally Harry breaks a pane of glass.

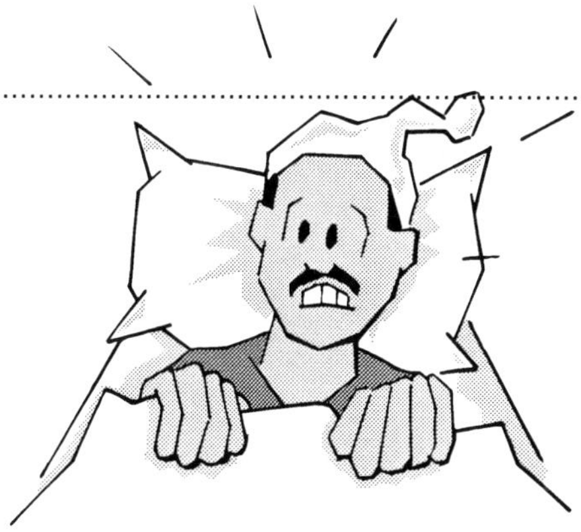

What a bad mistake!
The noise wakes up the Millers' neighbour, Mr. Watchit, who is a policeman by chance. Now the Millers are planning to install some further devices to make their house secure:

3. Burglar alarms

There are many burglar alarm systems now available, ranging from simple DIY kits to sophisticated electronic systems installed by special security firms. What you choose must be determined by your needs and lifestyle. The effectiveness of any alarm system is degraded if it's set off regularly by natural causes - like high winds and lightening - and neighbours can get annoyed by a less than perfect systems.

4. Security marking

Although marking you property is unlikely to stop it being stolen, you are at leats more likely to get it back. The police recover an enormous amount of stolen property and always have difficulty tracing the proper owners and it often ends up in another part of the country. The accepted marking is your postcode followed by the number of your house - or the first three letters of your house name if it doesn't have a number.

Security around the house

Lesson **3.13.3**

5. Security lightening

Front and back entrance doors should always be well lit; not only from the security point of view but for reasons of safety as well.

Timers and photo-electric cells can be wired into exterior and interior lights to switch them on and off while you are away.

Which devices do you have, or would you like to have in your house or flat?

Make 10 sentences like:

1. I have a *bell* on my door, because *visitors should ring.*
2. I wouldn't use a *rim latch*, because *it can easily be broken.*
3. I'd like to have a *door viewer*, because *you can check the identity of callers.*
4. I'd never install *an alarm system*, because *it is too expensive.*
5. ....
6. ....
7. *and so on ...*
8. ....
9. ....
10. ....

Is your house Elsafe?

Is your house Elsafe?

Beat the thief by installing a super-smart Elsafe M70 in your home or office

Operating the electronicElsafe is simple. Just enter a 6-digit code for your daily lie more convenient.

Worldwide, more than half a million Elsafes have beeb installed in offices, private homes and hotel rooms.

**Baht 19,990
INCLUDING VAT**

**Elsafe – the Norwegian-made, fully electronic safe.
Incorporating prize-winning technology.**

Make your home and office Elsafe and make your life easy

Call 259-8949 for Elsafe now!!!

Beat the thief.

Vocational education in Great Britain 1

After finishing school at the age of 15 or 16 (that´s the end of compulsory school education) some teenagers try and find unskilled work, others go to a College of Further Education in order to get their A-levels or a vocational training.

Most Colleges of Further Education offer a wide range of qualifications. Usually there is a comprehensive selection of A-level and GCSE programmes leading to entrance to universities and colleges of higher education, and to careers in industry, business or the professions.

Qualifications for vocational training are:

- **BTEC National Diploma:**

  These are two year programmes in a variety of subjects, providing the skills and knowledge needed for specific technical / professional jobs.

- **BTEC First Diploma:**
  These are one year training and educational programmes for students who know the particular field of work they want to enter but do not have the required qualifications for entry on to a BTEC National Diploma.

- **General National Vocational Qualifications (GNVQs):**
  GNVQs provide a broad-based vocational education and will eventually replace all BTEC First and National Diplomas. GNVQs do not lead directly to occupational competence. They offer the foundation of skills, knowledge and understanding which underpin a range of occupations or they lead to university entrance.

Vocational education in Great Britain 2

- National Vocational Qualifications (NVQs):

  These are qualifications about work, based on standards of competence set by industry. NVQ´s are awarded by established bodies such as RSA, City and Guilds, and BTEC. In 1986 the Government set up the National Council for Vocational Qualifications (NCVQ). This council has set out the structure and framework of NVQs. NVQs are nationally recognized qualifications related to job tasks. They describe the standards to which these tasks should be done and the knowledge needed to do it. NVQs are arranged in a hierarchy of 5 levels, from 1 (the most basic) to 5 (managerial and professional).

- Higher Education:Further on there are many more higher qualifications, leading to university entrance or to professional degrees.

Who pays?

In the UK the cost of industrial training is usually borne by industry.
A market research identified that in 1994/95

- a planned training was still rare in organisations with fewer than 25 employees;
- training was not equally available across all occupations;
- at least 20% of employees do nothing to plan or provide training.

Most courses offered by colleges of further education are usually free for 16 to 19 year olds. If you are over 19 the local Education Authority might pay the fees. Costs will vary depending on the number of lessons taken in one term. There are many different courses, eg. full-time, part-time (day and / or evening classes), weekend courses and so on. The duration of these courses depend on the qualification you want to achieve.

Notizen

I. Verbs for metal work used in exercise 2 (page 41)

to be driven – angetrieben werden

to clamp together – zusammen klemmen

to cut – schneiden

to do up – anziehen (Schraube)

to fit – einpassen

to grind – schleifen, schärfen

to grip – fest halten

to join – verbinden

to loosen – lösen

to need – benötigen

to range – hier: erhältich sein, zu finden sein

to replace – austauschen, ersetzen

to remove – abnehmen, ausbauen

to sand – schleifen

to saw – sägen

to sharpen – schärfen

to tighten – fest machen

to turn – drehen

to undo – lösen (Schraube)

II. Computers 2 (page 18)

1. *E-mail <u>is used</u> to communicate world-wide within seconds.*
2. *Navigation systems in cars <u>are used</u> to reach a certain destination very quickly.*
3. *In Computer Aided Design <u>you can make</u> alterations of drawings easily.*
4. *LAN <u>is needed</u> for quick communications within companies.*

Notizen

III. How to use a soldering iron (page 47) *(ebenso als Arbeitsanweisung – instructions – möglich.)*

1. *First the soldering iron must be connected to the mains supply.*
2. *Then the wires can be joined and twisted by hand.*
3. *Next the joint must be heated by the soldering iron.*
4. *Then the solder should be melted with the soldering iron.*
5. *Next the joint must be covered with the liquid solder.*
6. *Then the soldering iron should be replaced on its stand.*
7. *Finally the plug must be removed from the socket.*

IV. Verbs for plumbing used in exercise 2 (page 54)

to be achieved	*erreicht haben*	*to hold*	*halten*
to be available	*erhältlich sein*	*to isolate*	*isolieren*
to be matching	*passend sein*	*to join*	*verbinden*
to bend	*biegen*	*to need*	*benötigen*
to clean	*säubern*	*to operate*	*bedienen*
to deliver	*herausgeben*	*to provide*	*zur Verfügung stellen/versorgen*
to ensure	*sich versichern*	*to put around*	*herumlegen*
to fall	*fallen*	*to remove*	*entfernen*
to feed	*nachfüllen*	*to sense*	*aufspüren*
to find	*herausfinden*	*to undo*	*lösen*
to fit	*einpassen*	*to use*	*benutzen*

Notizen

Translation exercise (Nr. 4) from page 56

1. *The water tap should be shiny.*
2. *The shower curtain should be clean.*
3. *Water should spray from the shower head.*
4. *You should be able to place the soap somewhere.*
5. *You should be able to see yourself in the mirror.*
6. *The tiles shoud be replaced.*
7. *The wall paint should be renewed.*
8. *You should always be careful.*
9. *The water tap should be easy to turn.*
10. *The bathroom should not smell bad.*
11. *You shouldn't leave anything around.*
12. *You should only pour liquids into the drain.*
13. *You should buy a new bath mat.*
14. *You should clear/clean the pipes.*
15. *Everything should look new.*

How to make good use of the various toolboxes

Step 1: Choose one of the tasks and make a list of all the tools you need for this job.

e.g. installing a sink, repairing an electric fan, erecting a brick wall, building a computer table, installing a thermostatic valve, fixing a blocked trap, repairing a blown socket ... many more possible

Step 2: Explain why you need the chosen tools.

e.g. I need the cramp for holding the workpieces together.
I need the mains tester to check if appliances are live. (...)

Step 3: Describe how you are going to accomplish your job.

or

Give instructions to your working mate who has never done this job before.

Notizen

Vocab Test A

Name

Klasse

1	1–	2+	2	2–	3+	3	3–	4+	4	4–	5+	5	5–	6	0
50,49	48,47	46-45	44-42	41-40	39-38	37-35	34-33	32-31	30-28	27-26	25-24	23-21	20-19	19-0	

Vocab Test B

Name
Klasse

1	1–	2+	2	2–	3+	3	3–	4+	4	4–	5+	5	5–	6	0
50,49	48,47	46-45	44-42	41-40	39-38	37-35	34-33	32-31	30-28	27-26	25-24	23-21	20-19	19-0	

Vocab Test A

Engines
Name
Klasse

Achse			pollutant		
Boden			pressure		
Bürsten			service		
Nockenwelle			slit		
Katalysator			spark plug		
coil			Takt		
combustion			winzig		
commutator			erlauben, lassen		
compression			angetrieben werden		
condenser			verbrennen		
Kurbelwelle			vervollständigen		
Strom			to compress		
Verteiler			to escape		
Ausstoß			to expand		
Auspuff			to fix		
exhaust valve			to ignite		
flywheel			einspitzen		
fuel chamber			produzieren		
ignition			lösen		
inlet valve			abstoßen		
Einlass			sich drehen		
Magnetfeld			to suck		
Wartung			to travel		
gegensätzlich			top		
Dauermagnet			wire		

1	1–	2+	2	2–	3+	3	3–	4+	4	4–	5+	5	5–	6	0
50,49	48,47	46-45	44-42	41-40	39-38	37-35	34-33	32-31	30-28	27-26	25-24	23-21	20-19	19-0	

Vocab Test B

Engines	
Name	
Klasse	

bottom			Druck		
brushes			Wartung		
camshaft			Schlitz		
catalytic converter			Zündkerze		
coil			Takt		
Verbrennung			tiny		
Kommutator			to allow		
Verdichtung			to be driven		
Verdichter			to cause		
Kondensator			to combust		
crankshaft			vervollständigen		
current			verdichten		
distributer			entweichen		
emission			sich ausdehnen		
exhaust			fixieren		
Schwungrad			to inject		
Vorläufer			to invent		
Brennstoffkammer			to produce		
Zündung			to release		
Einlassventil			to repel		
jet			herumdrehen		
magnetic field			einsaugen		
maintenance			strömen		
nozzle			gebrauchen		
permanent magnet			Draht		

1	1–	2+	2	2–	3+	3	3–	4+	4	4–	5+	5	5–	6	0
50,49	48,47	46-45	44-42	41-40	39-38	37-35	34-33	32-31	30-28	27-26	25-24	23-21	20-19	19-0	

Vocab Test A

Computers

Name

Klasse

output			streamer		
beinhalten			Schnittstelle		
einlesen			Speicherung		
to store			batch file		
access			delivery		
vermehren			pad		
lösen			Verzeichnis		
Fertigung			Drucker		
recognition			Erkennung		
Eingabe			research		
to fit			to reset		
sammeln			to retrieve		
verarbeiten			auswählen		
scanner			to influence		
Laufwerk			herstellen		
to emit			integriert		
übermitteln			capacity		
speichern			Bildschirm		
Nachricht			benötigen		
joy-stick			to calculate		
Speicher			Daten eigeben		
verbessern			Datei		
to design			unterstützt		
überprüfen			to retrieve		
to create			plotter		

1	1–	2+	2	2–	3+	3	3–	4+	4	4–	5+	5	5–	6	0
50,49	48,47	46-45	44-42	41-40	39-38	37-35	34-33	32-31	30-28	27-26	25-24	23-21	20-19	19-0	

Vocab Test B

Computers

Name

Klasse

zurückstellen			Kapazität		
to multiply			erschaffen		
Stapeldatei			hinein passen		
message			file		
drive			Drucker		
hardware			Zugang		
Forschung			to store		
entwerfen			verdeutlichen		
to scan			Zeichengerät		
ausstrahlen			to retrieve		
beeinflussen			Übergabe		
lösen			interface		
simulieren			recognition		
to translate			input		
verändern			Glasfaser		
monitor			Prozessor		
memory			Richtpodell		
directory			Tastatur		
to check			to process		
Daten eingeben			to transmit		
to select			berechnen		
streamer			to require		
Fertigung			beinhalten		
Lesegerät			Unterlage		
Schaltknüppel			aided		

1	1–	2+	2	2–	3+	3	3–	4+	4	4–	5+	5	5–	6	0
50,49	48,47	46-45	44-42	41-40	39-38	37-35	34-33	32-31	30-28	27-26	25-24	23-21	20-19	19-0	

Vocab Test A

Electricity

Name

Klasse

cable drum			Draht		
to check			to plug in		
to twist			schneiden		
meter			to distribute		
unter Strom			messen		
Kneifzange			Schalter		
socket			sheathing		
rewirable			isoliert		
Sicherung			Unterputzdose		
Verbindung			conductor		
to bend			iron core		
mounted			Aufnahmegerät		
to strip			einpassen		
bulb			available		
Geräte			fittings		
Stecker			torch		
strips			to attach		
to fix			laut stellen		
ausschalten			Widerstand		
Hauptschalter			Spannungsprüfer		
Kneifzange			device		
Klemmschraube			Strom		
Stromkreis			cable clip		
flex			aufheben		
Stromversorgung			Adapter		

1	1–	2+	2	2–	3+	3	3–	4+	4	4–	5+	5	5–	6	0
50,49	48,47	46-45	44-42	41-40	39-38	37-35	34-33	32-31	30-28	27-26	25-24	23-21	20-19	19-0	

Vocab Test B

Electricity

Name

Klasse

adapter			leiser machen		
wieder verdrahtbar			drehen		
to examine			Taschenlampe		
erhältlich			wire		
Zähler			einstöpseln		
Kabel verlegen			switch		
to connect			to pick up		
to switch off			built-in		
appliances			cable channel		
clamp			circuit		
Verbrauch			connections		
Strom			DIY		
biegen			to measure		
verteilen			to turn up		
Streifen			to unplug		
Steckdose			terminal block		
Glühlampe			Isolierung		
Vorrichtung			Kabeltrommel		
Eisenkern			resistance		
nippers			to insert		
plug			recorder		
to cut			live		
outlet			fuse		
mains			insulated		
befestigt			Leiter		

1	1–	2+	2	2–	3+	3	3–	4+	4	4–	5+	5	5–	6	0
50,49	48,47	46-45	44-42	41-40	39-38	37-35	34-33	32-31	30-28	27-26	25-24	23-21	20-19	19-0	

Vocab Test A

Welding and soldering

Name

Klasse

schweißen			alloy		
brass			Unfall		
Strom			tip		
flux			gelagert werden		
Blei			to insulate		
goggles			to discolour		
Druckanzeiger			thickness		
Lötmetall			to adjust		
beschaffen			gut isoliert		
to prevent			copper		
to melt			verschmelzen		
sich auflösen			Schweißhandschuhe		
verdichten			spark		
combustable			Schmiermittel		
Beton			filler metal		
pressure regulator			welding torch		
Elektroschock			to be supplied		
face mask			to be composed of		
soldering			joint		
Ventil			Schlauch		
Werkstück			Feuerlöscher		
to vaporise			Lichtbogen		
welding rod			Barriere		
powerful			überhitzen		
Schürze			Gasflasche		

1	1–	2+	2	2–	3+	3	3–	4+	4	4–	5+	5	5–	6	0
50,49	48,47	46-45	44-42	41-40	39-38	37-35	34-33	32-31	30-28	27-26	25-24	23-21	20-19	19-0	

Vocab Test B

Welding and soldering

Name

Klasse

accident			appropriate		
tin			barrier		
Funke			grease		
Spitze			hydrogen		
einstellen			Löten		
to be stored			Dicke		
concrete			to dissolve		
Kupfer			workpiece		
valve			Messing		
lead (metal)			earth clamp		
Gasfluss			Schweissstab		
hose			Leiter (elektr.)		
to weld			Flussmittel		
well-insulated			brennbar		
to overheat			Verbindung		
to compress			to fuse		
Bronze			Druckregulator		
Legierung			welding gloves		
arc			vorbeugen		
Maske			schmelzen		
Füllmetall			apron		
Sauerstoff			sich verfärben		
solder			to provide		
pressure gauge			verflüchtigen		
isolieren			bestehen aus		

1	1–	2+	2	2–	3+	3	3–	4+	4	4–	5+	5	5–	6	0
50,49	48,47	46-45	44-42	41-40	39-38	37-35	34-33	32-31	30-28	27-26	25-24	23-21	20-19	19-0	

Crossword – Translation D-E

ENGINES

Across:

1 Druck
2. Unterseite
9. Matte
10. sich drehen
11. Schale, Pokal
12. Aufgabe
14. z.B.
15. antreiben
19. amerikanische Autofirma
22. Düse, Mündung
23. Stamm
24. sehr teure Brandymarke
25. sich bewegen (Kolben)
26. zerfressen (Rost)
27. Nockenwelle
31. Achse
32. verwenden
35. Tiegel, Gefäß
36. sich festfressen (Kolben)
37. Einlass
44. sich drehen
48. Bezeichnung für Arbeitsspeicher
49. Gerundium von „besuchen"

1		3	40	18		16	43	2	4	5	6	7	8
		9											
10	42				17		11						
12													
						13							
			45			49				20		14	
15		19						23					
21		22							26				
24			25							44			
				27			33			47			
31			46		36						28		
32	34							38	41			29	
				37		39							30
	35				48								

Down:

1. Kolben
2. Bürsten
3. Ausstoß
4. gegenläufige (Kolben)
5. winzig
6. Röhre
7. entgegengesetzt
8. Wartung
11. Umhang
16. loslassen
17. Oberteil
18. Takt (Maschine)
20. sauber, ordentlich, rein
21. Auspuff
28. ansaugen (Luft- Gasgemisch)
29. befestigen, reparieren
30. Kurzform für Gleichstrom
33. Dampf
34. Zapfen, Wasserhahn
38. kurze Zustimmung
39. zu, hin
40. Vergangenheit von „untergehen"
41. Strahlrohr
42. Papier
43. entweichen (Dampf)
45. Stelle, Punkt
46. Schlitz, Spalt
47. Brennstoff

Crossword – one spelling mistake to be found **COMPUTERS**

Across:

1. gained after password
6. connection to internet
9. drawing program
10. opposite: direct current
11. to read s.th. into the computer
12. American internet supplier
13. data to be used
14. track for mouse
16. short form: number
17. valve for electrical current
18. preposition
19. finding the way in the net
21. essential for every engine
22. device for identification of data
23. to gain data
25. around the wheel
27. short form: personal computer
28. tool to type in texts
30. program used for designing
31. connects all electric components
33. to move about in the net
34. never forget when leaving your beloved
35. to recycle
37. short form: for example
39. place of water in the desert
40. smallest unit storable
42. very important

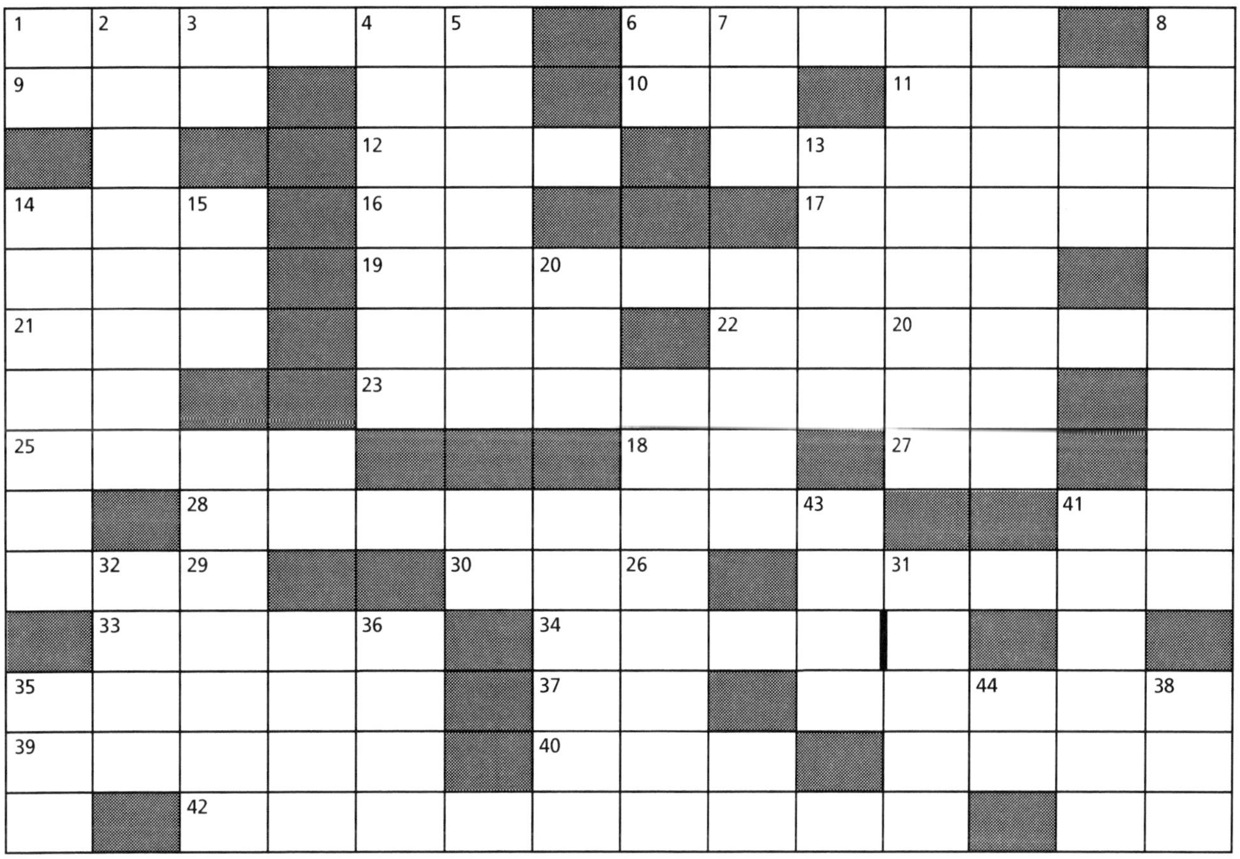

Down:

1. short form: artificial climate
2. condition of computer
3. medium to file data
4. device to read in pictures
5. saving of data
7. indicating lamp (short)
8. device making transmission possible
14. drawing device for large drawings
15. opposite: to save (short form)
20. tax added in GB
26. very small unit
29. used to move the curser
31. used for steering
32. local ... network
35. stored data
36. happens when you are not alert
38. computer program for manufacturing
41. to make up
43. used for storing
44. opposite: alternating current

Crossword ELECTRICITY

Across:

1. Anschlussstelle
2. Draht
7. Aufnahmegerät
9. (Sicherheitsbestimmungen)
10. Taschenlampe
11. Klemme
12. isolieren
13. befestigen
14. Zeichenprogramm
15. abisolieren
16. Sicherung
17. verbinden
18. innerhalb
20. Kneifzange
24. dünnes Kabel
25. Hinweise
26. z.B.
27. erhalten
28. unter Strom
31. Hauptschalter
32. wieder verdrahtbar
33. Adapter
35. Blech

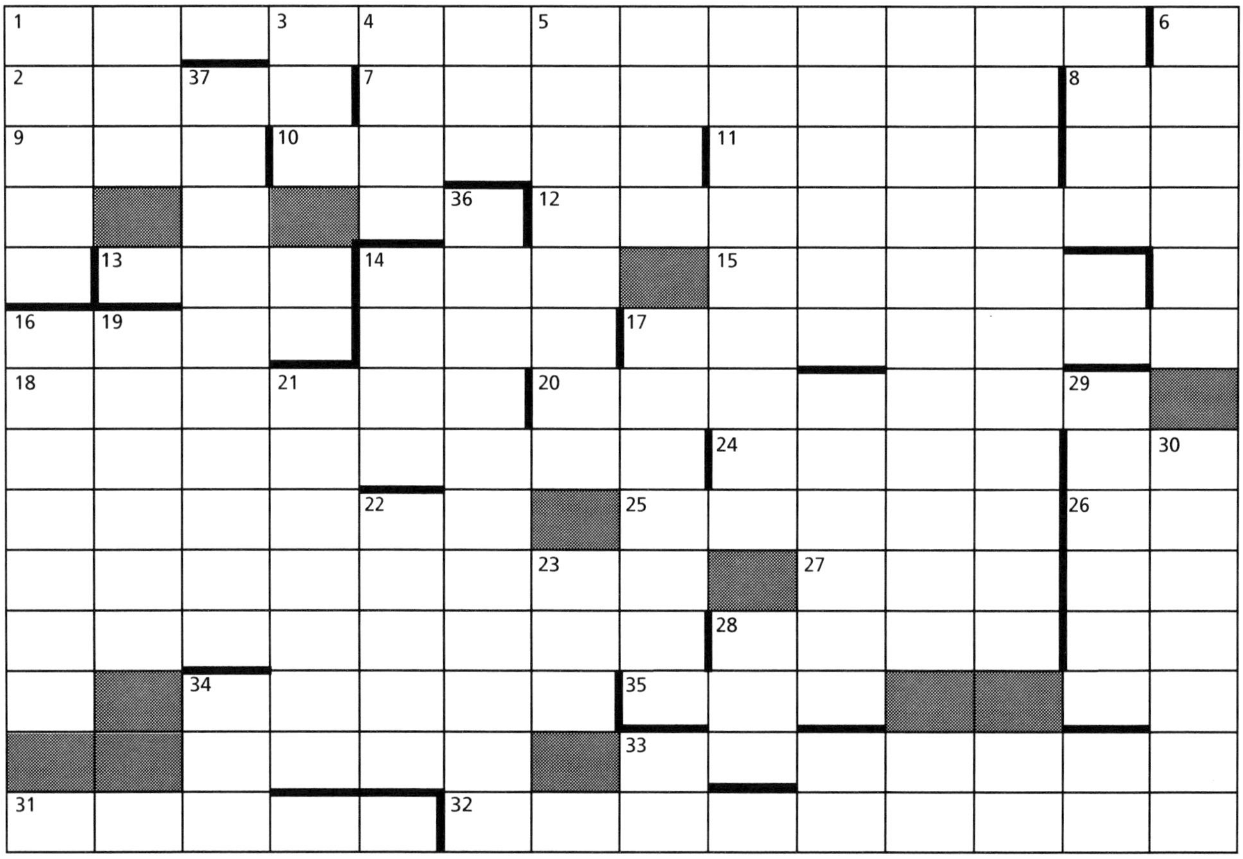

Down:

1. drehen
4. Eisen
5. Unfall
6. hinein legen
8. schneiden
14. Kern
16. Passung
17. Stromkreis
19. ausschalten
21. untersuchen
22. Fackel, Taschenlampe
23. schneiden
28. Deckel
29. Schalter
30. messen
34. Männername
36. Spannungsprüfer
37. Widerstand

Crossword — WELDING AND SOLDERING

Across:

1. kräftig
2. Messing
3. Weizen
4. schweißen
5. Erdungsklammer
6. z.B.
7. engl. Adelstitel
8. Lötmetall
9. Sauerstoff
10. isolieren
11. Schmiermittel
12. sparsam
13. zugehörig
14. Lichtbogen
29. schmelzen
33. Gleichstrom
35. Grube
36. einsaugen
37. Leuchtdiode
38. Hohlform, Gussform (USA)
39. klemmen
40. kaputt machen
41. Zinn

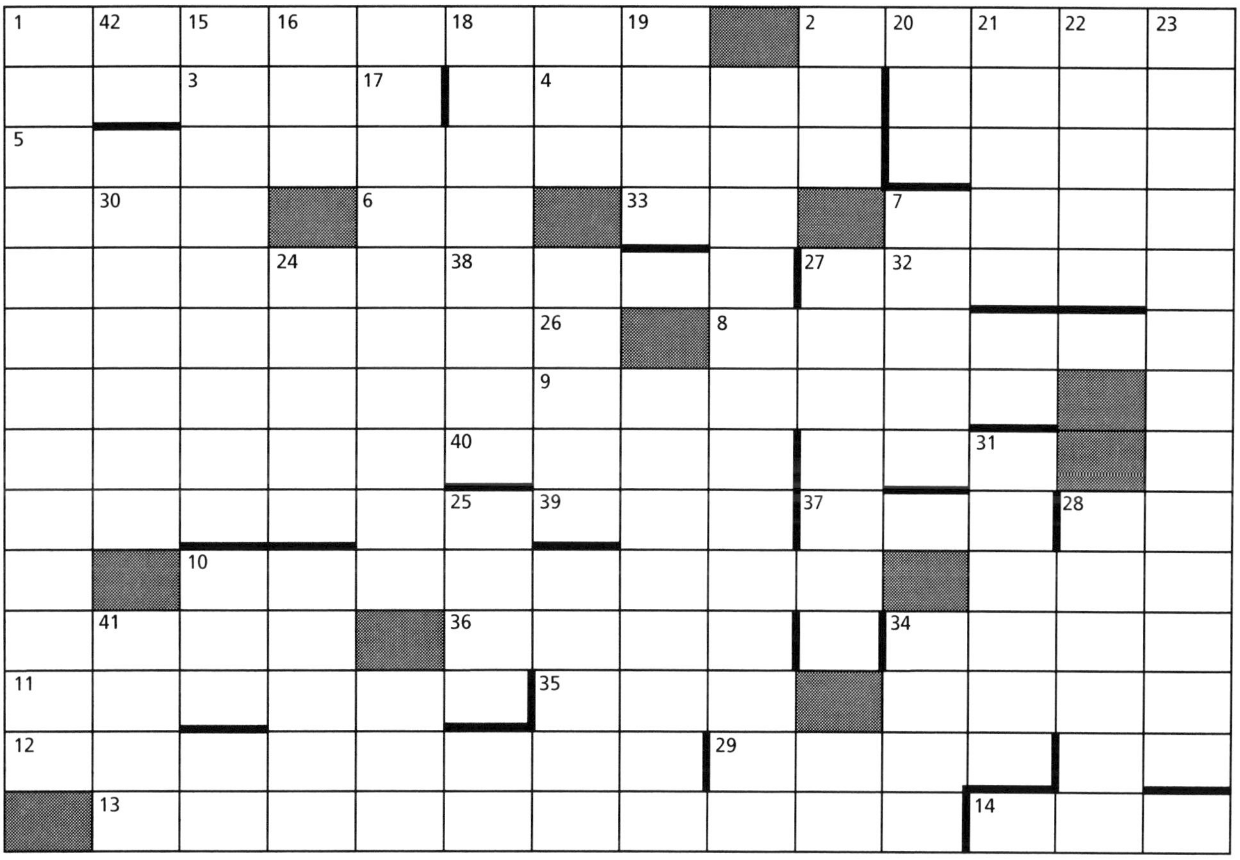

Down:

1. Druckanzeiger
15. Werkstück
16. zerfressen (Rost)
17. Dicke
18. Gesichtsmaske
19. Blei
20. Stab
21. Schürze
22. Funke
23. Lötkolben
24. Ventil
25. verschmelzen
26. verbinden
27. Schutzbrille
28. sich färben
30. einschalten
31. einstellen
32. dünnes Kabel
34. Insel
42. eingeschaltet

Lösung – gilt für „Crossword“ und „search-a-word“

ENGINES

1 P	R	3 E	40 S	18 S	U	16 R	43 E	2 B	4 O	5 T	6 T	7 O	8 M
I		9 M	A	T		E	S	R	P	I	U	P	A
10 S	42 P	I	N	R	17 T	L	11 C	U	P	N	B	P	I
12 T	A	S	K	O	O	E	A	S	O	Y	E	O	N
O	P	S		K	P	13 A	P	H	S			S	T
N	E	I	45 S	E		49 S	E	E	I	20 N	G	14 I	E
15 P	R	19 O	P	E	L	E		23 S	T	E	M	T	N
21 E		22 N	O	Z	Z	L	E		26 E	A	T	E	A
24 X	O		25 T	R	A	V	E	L		44 T	U	R	N
H				27 C	A	M	33 S	H	A	47 F	T		C
31 A	X	I	46 S		36 P	I	T			U	28 S		E
32 U	34 T	I	L	I	S	E	E	38 O	41 J	E	U	29 F	
S	A		I	37 I	N	39 T	A	K	E	L	C	I	30 D
T	35 P	O	T		48 R	O	M		T		K	X	C

COMPUTERS

1 A	2 C	3 C	E	4 S	5 S		6 M	7 O	D	E	M		8 I	
9 C	A	D		C	T		10 A	C		11 S	C	A	N	
	P			12 A	O	L		R	13 I	N	P	U	T	
14 P	A	15 D		16 N	R				17 D	I	O	D	E	
L	C	E		19 N	A	20 V	I	G	A	T	E		R	
21 O	I	L		E	G	A		22 R	E	20 A	D	E	R	*MISTAKE*
T	T			23 R	E	T	R	I	E	V	E		F	
25 T	Y	R	E				18 O	N		27 P	C		A	
E		28 K	E	Y	B	O	A	R	43 D			41 C	C	
R	32 A	29 M			30 C	A	26 D		I	31 W	I	R	E	
	33 R	O	A	36 M		34 K	I	S	S	H		E		
35 R	E	U	S	E		37 E	G		C	E	44 D	A	38 C	
39 O	A	S	I	S		40 B	I	T		E	C	T	I	
M		42 E	S	S	E	N	T	I	A	L		E	M	

Lösung

ELECTRICITY

1 T	E	R	3 M	4 I	N	5 A	L	B	L	O	C	K	6 I
2 W	I	37 R	E	7 R	E	C	O	R	D	E	R	8 C	N
9 I	E	E	10 T	O	R	C	H	11 C	L	I	P	U	S
S		S		N	36 M	12 I	N	S	U	L	A	T	E
T	13 F	I	X	14 C	A	D		15 S	T	R	I	P	R
16 F	19 U	S	E	O	I	E	17 C	O	N	N	E	C	T
18 I	N	T	21 E	R	N	20 N	I	P	P	E	R	29 S	
T	P	A	X	E	S	T	R	24 F	L	E	X	W	30 M
T	L	N	A	22 T	T		25 C	L	U	E	S	26 I	E
I	U	C	M	O	E	23 C	U		27 G	E	T	T	A
N	G	E	I	R	S	U	I	28 L	I	V	E	C	S
G		34 A	N	C	T	T	35 T	I	N			H	U
		L	E	H	E		33 A	D	A	P	T	E	R
31 M	A	I	N	S	32 R	E	W	I	R	A	B	L	E

WELDING AND SOLDERING

1 P	42 O	15 W	16 E	R	18 F	U	19 L		2 B	20 R	21 A	22 S	23 S
R	N	3 O	A	17 T	A	4 W	E	L	D	O	P	P	O
5 E	A	R	T	H	C	L	A	M	P	D	R	A	L
S	30 T	K		6 I	E		33 D	C		7 L	O	R	D
S	U	P	24 V	C	38 M	O	L	D	27 G	32 F	N	K	E
U	R	I	A	K	A	26 J		8 S	O	L	D	E	R
R	N	E	L	N	S	9 O	X	Y	G	E	N		I
E	O	C	V	E	40 K	I	L	L	G	X	31 A		N
G	N	E	E	S	25 F	39 N	I	P	37 L	E	D	28 C	G
A		10 I	N	S	U	L	A	T	E		J	O	I
U	41 T	I	N		36 S	U	C	K	S	34 I	U	L	R
11 G	R	E	A	S	E	35 P	I	T		S	S	O	O
12 E	C	O	N	O	M	I	C	29 M	E	L	T	U	N
	13 A	P	R	O	P	R	I	A	T	E	14 A	R	C

Search a word – only down and across

- 52 items to be found **ENGINES**

P	R	E	S	S	U	R	E	B	O	T	T	O	M
I	T	M	A	T	F	E	S	R	P	I	U	P	A
S	P	I	N	R	T	L	C	U	P	N	B	P	I
T	A	S	K	O	O	E	A	S	O	Y	E	O	N
O	P	S	T	K	P	A	P	H	S	L	L	S	T
N	E	I	S	E	K	S	E	E	I	N	G	I	E
P	R	O	P	E	L	E	H	S	T	E	M	T	N
E	T	N	O	Z	Z	L	E	N	E	A	T	E	A
X	O	G	T	R	A	V	E	L	H	T	U	R	N
H	G	B	N	C	A	M	S	H	A	F	T	L	C
A	X	I	S	V	P	I	T	B	M	U	S	L	E
U	T	I	L	I	S	E	E	O	J	E	U	F	L
S	A	E	I	I	N	T	A	K	E	L	C	I	D
T	P	O	T	E	R	O	M	T	T	T	K	X	C

- 47 items to be found **COMPUTERS**

A	C	C	E	S	S	T	M	O	D	E	M	T	I
C	A	D	F	C	T	Z	A	C	S	S	C	A	N
N	P	T	N	A	O	L	L	R	I	N	P	V	T
P	A	D	K	N	R	N	T	M	D	I	O	D	E
L	C	E	S	N	A	V	I	G	A	T	E	S	R
O	I	L	S	E	G	A	S	R	E	A	D	E	R
T	T	W	R	R	E	T	R	I	E	V	E	J	F
T	Y	R	E	N	M	W	O	N	B	P	C	J	A
E	A	K	E	Y	B	O	A	R	D	F	A	C	C
R	A	M	S	E	C	A	D	I	I	W	I	R	E
E	R	O	A	M	D	K	I	S	S	H	H	E	O
R	E	U	S	E	H	E	G	H	C	E	D	A	C
O	A	S	I	S	N	B	I	T	H	E	C	T	I
M	H	E	S	S	E	N	T	I	A	L	H	E	M

Search a word – only down and across

- *41 items to be found* **ELECTRICITY**

T	E	R	M	I	N	A	L	B	L	O	C	K	I
W	I	R	E	R	E	C	O	R	D	E	R	C	N
I	E	E	T	O	R	C	H	C	L	I	P	U	S
S	H	S	H	N	M	I	N	S	U	L	A	T	E
T	F	I	X	C	A	D	H	S	T	R	I	P	R
F	U	S	E	O	I	E	C	O	N	N	E	C	T
I	N	T	E	R	N	N	I	P	P	E	R	S	H
T	P	A	X	E	S	T	R	F	L	E	X	W	M
T	L	N	A	T	T	H	C	L	U	E	S	I	E
I	U	C	M	O	E	C	U	T	G	E	T	T	A
N	G	E	I	R	S	U	I	L	I	V	E	C	S
G	S	A	N	C	T	T	T	I	N	B	B	H	U
CB	C	L	E	H	E	T	A	D	A	P	T	E	R
M	A	I	N	S	R	E	W	I	R	A	B	L	E

- *43 items to be found* **WELDING**

P	O	W	E	R	F	U	L	G	B	R	A	S	S
R	N	O	A	T	A	W	E	L	D	O	P	P	O
E	A	R	T	H	C	L	A	M	P	D	R	A	L
S	T	K	FF	I	E	F	D	C	G	L	O	R	D
S	U	P	V	C	M	O	L	D	G	F	N	K	E
U	R	I	A	K	A	J	G	S	O	L	D	E	R
R	N	E	L	N	S	O	X	Y	G	E	N	Q	I
E	O	C	V	E	K	I	L	L	G	X	A	M	N
G	N	E	E	S	F	N	I	P	L	E	D	C	G
A	S	I	N	S	U	L	A	T	E	F	J	O	I
U	T	I	N		S	U	C	K	S	I	U	L	R
G	R	E	A	S	E	P	I	T	F	S	S	O	O
E	C	O	N	O	M	I	C	M	E	L	T	U	N
	A	P	R	O	P	R	I	A	T	E	A	R	C

1. Thomas Newcomen (1663-1729)

2. Slide Valve

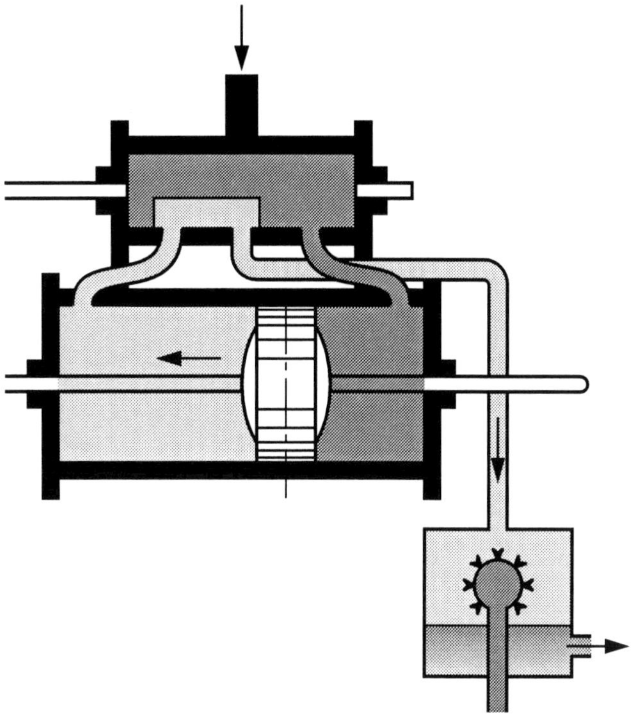

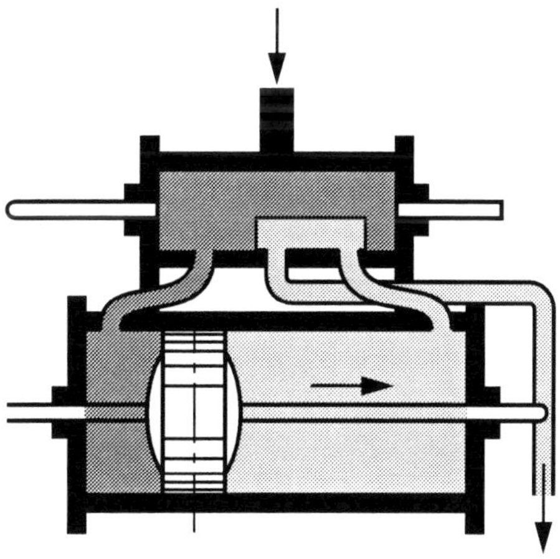

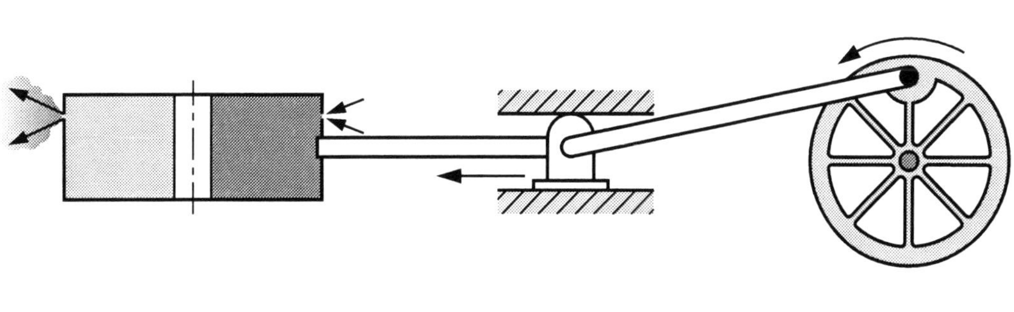

3. Four-Stroke Petrol Engine

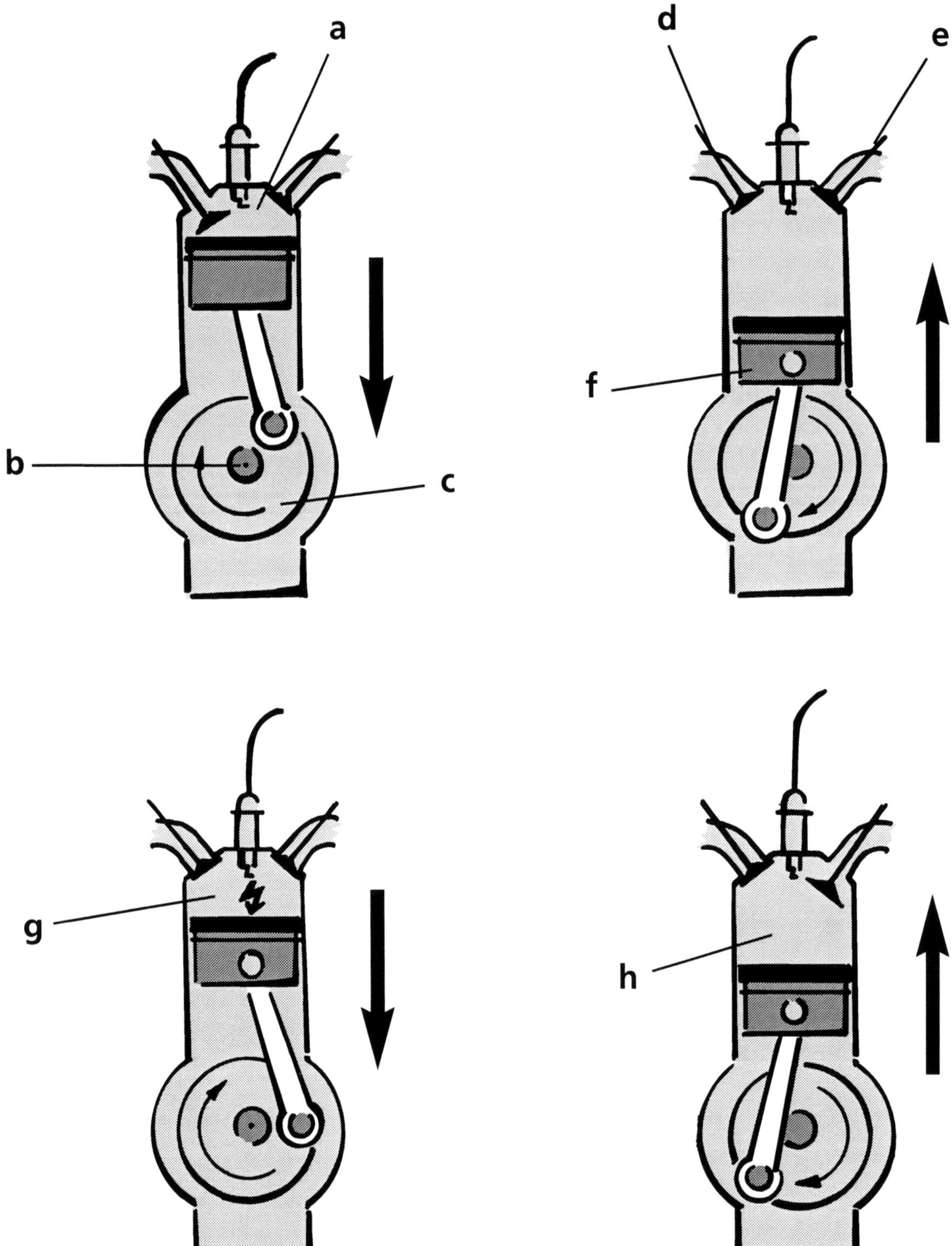

4. Electric Motor

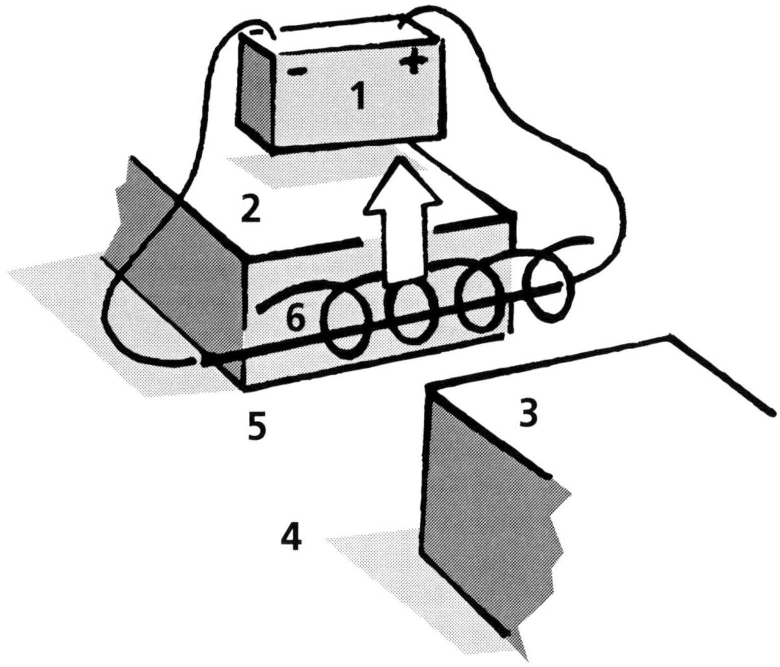

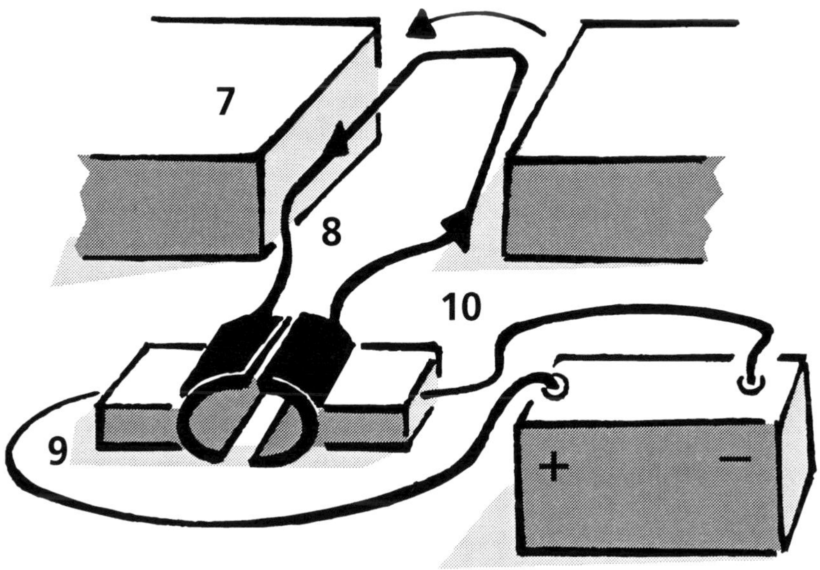

5. Computers – Basic Elements

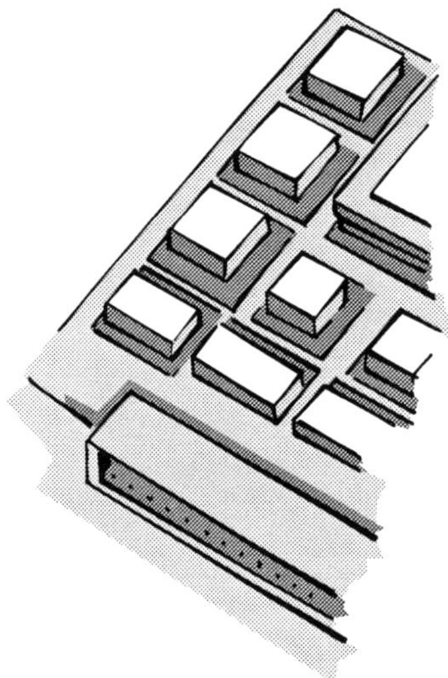

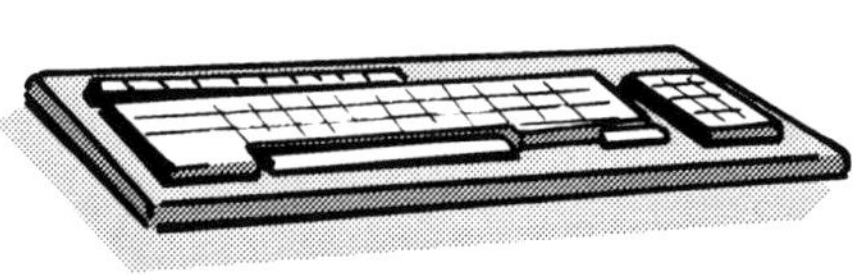
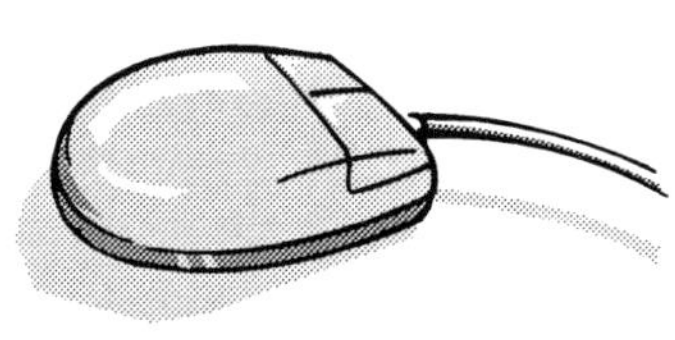

6. Computerized Design and Production

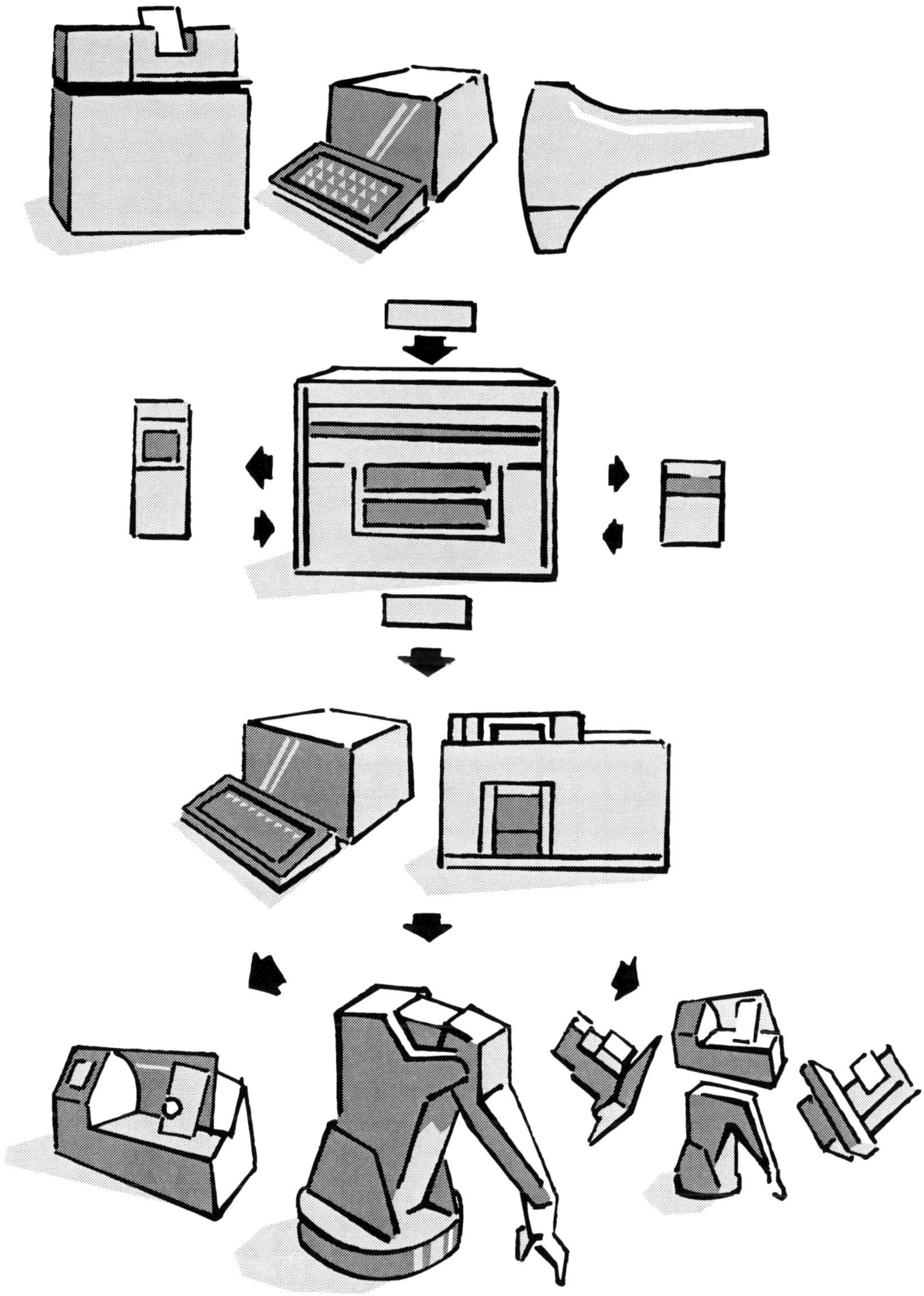

7. Welding

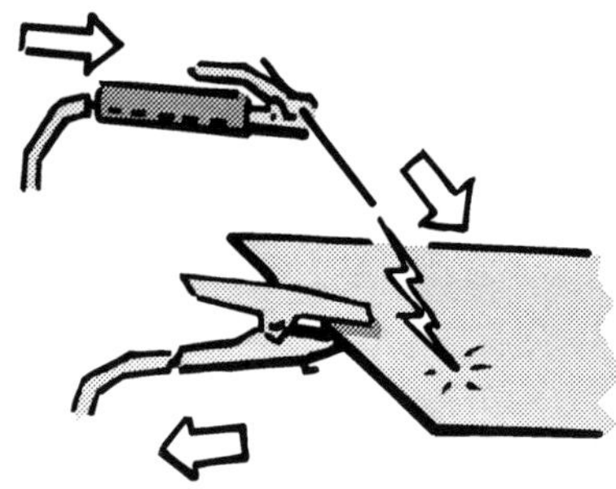

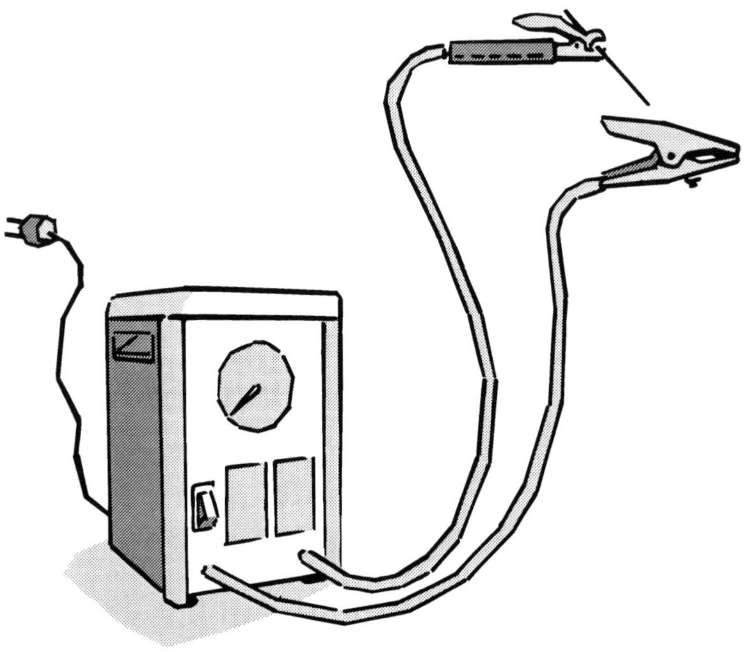

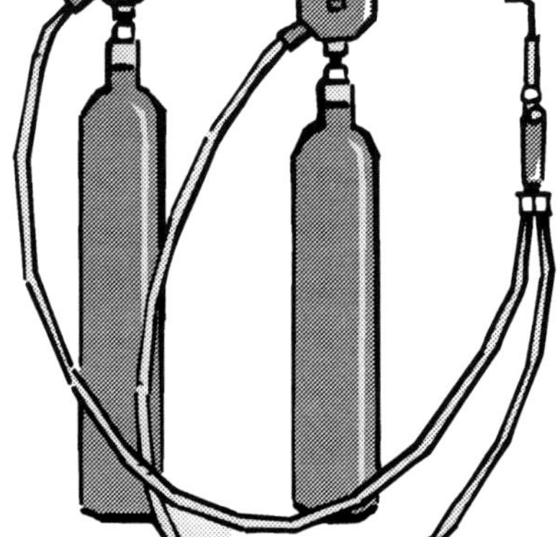

8. The Bathroom – spick-and-span

Toolbox 1 – Electricity

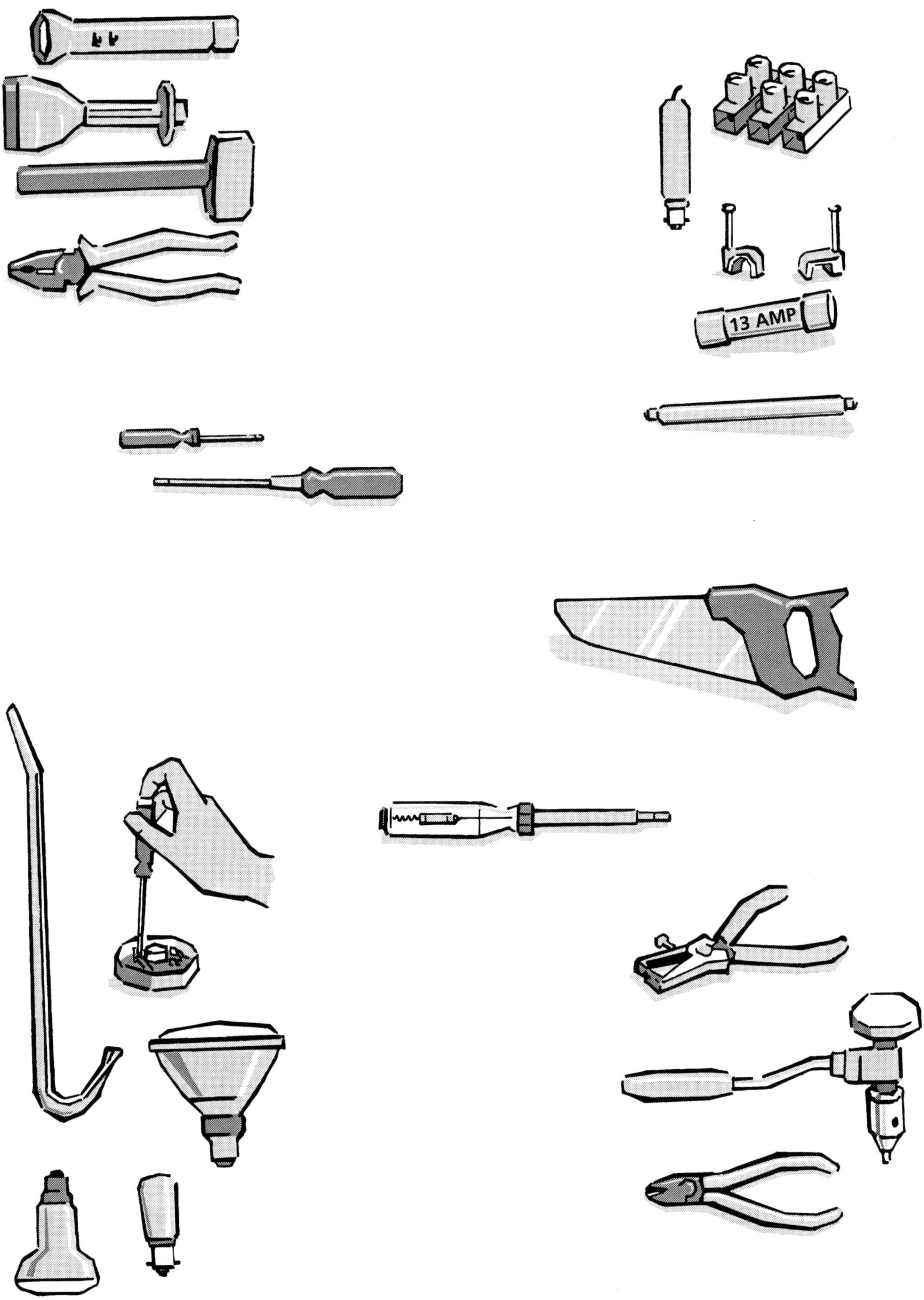

Toolbox 2 – Metalwork

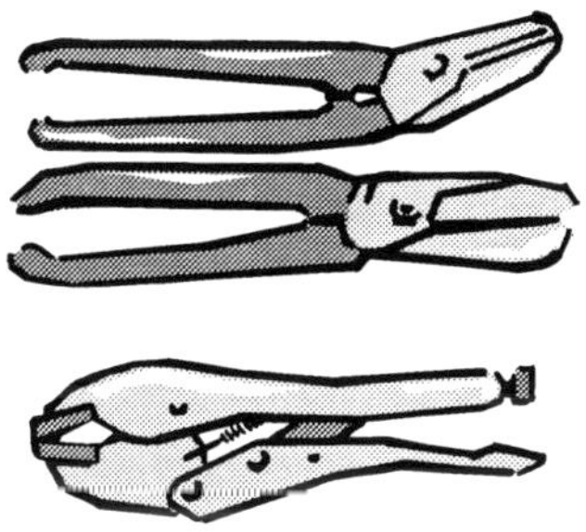
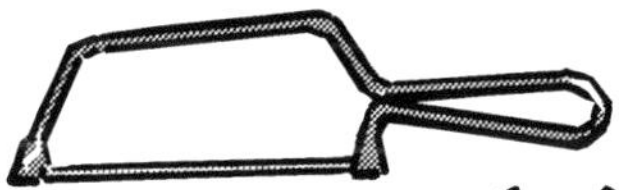
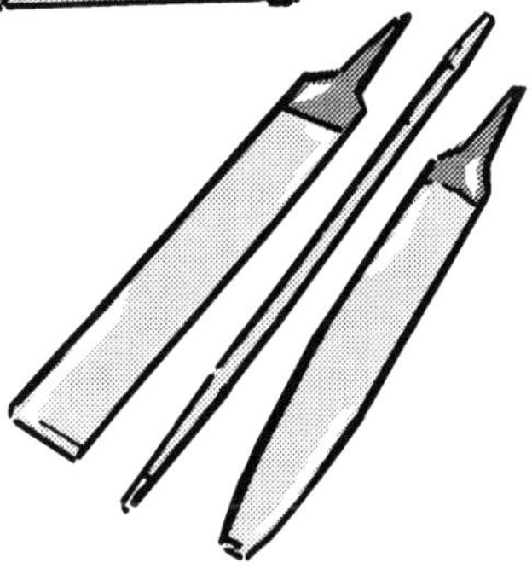
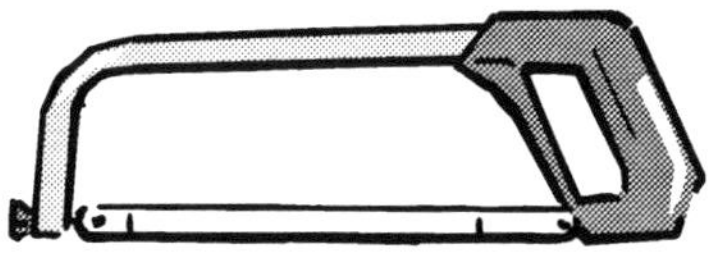

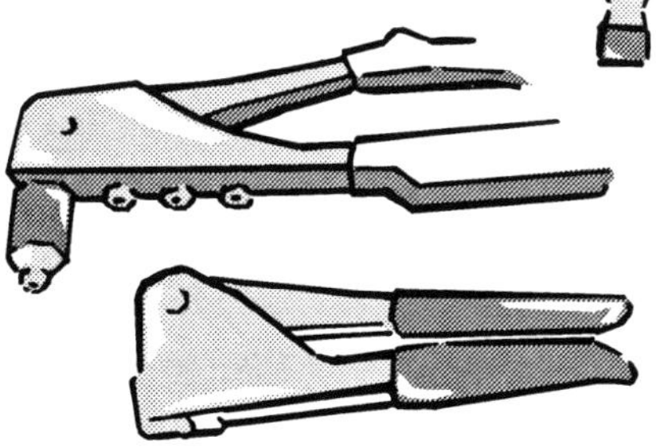

Toolbox 3 – Plumbing

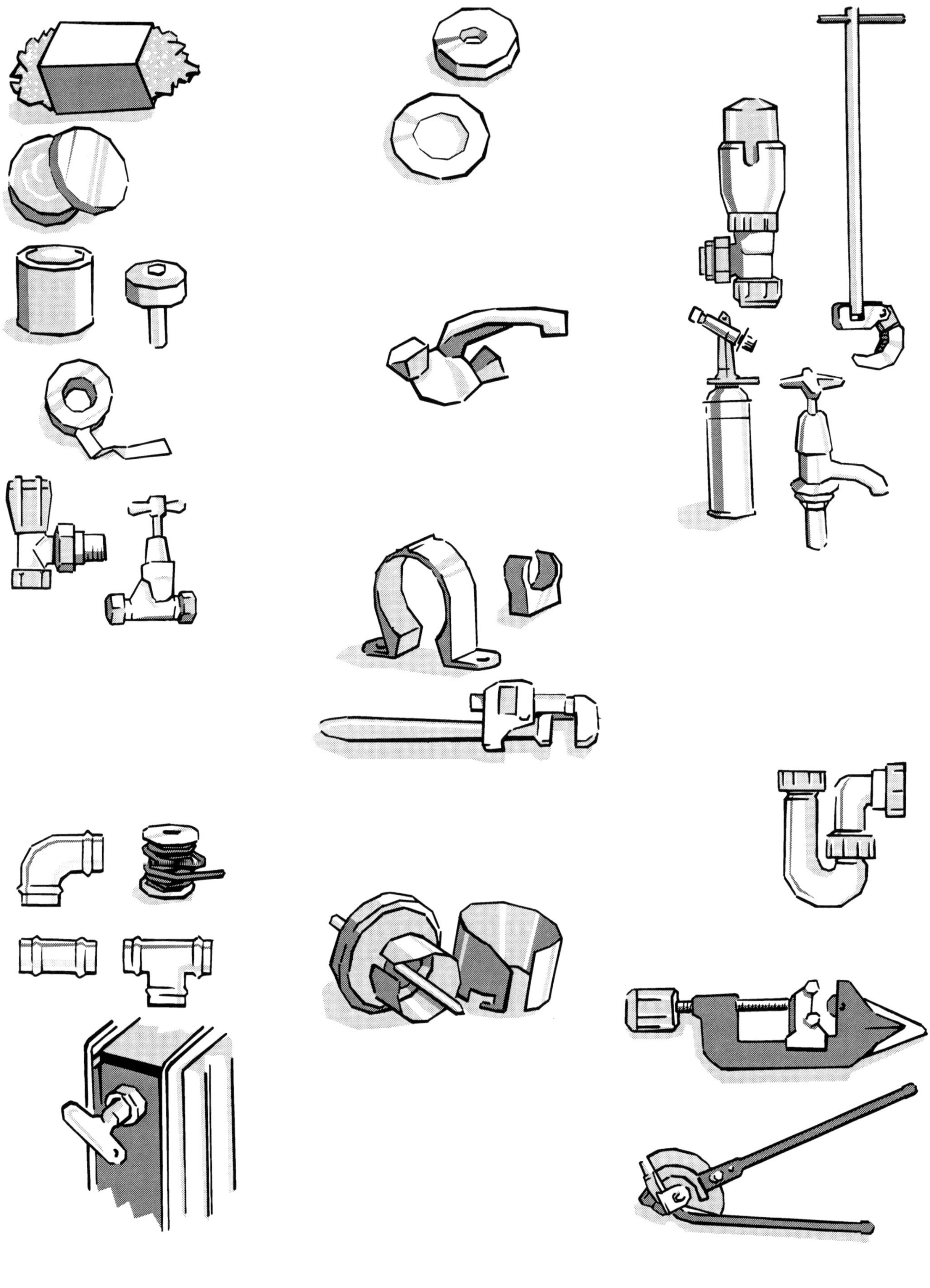

Toolbox 4 – Woodwork

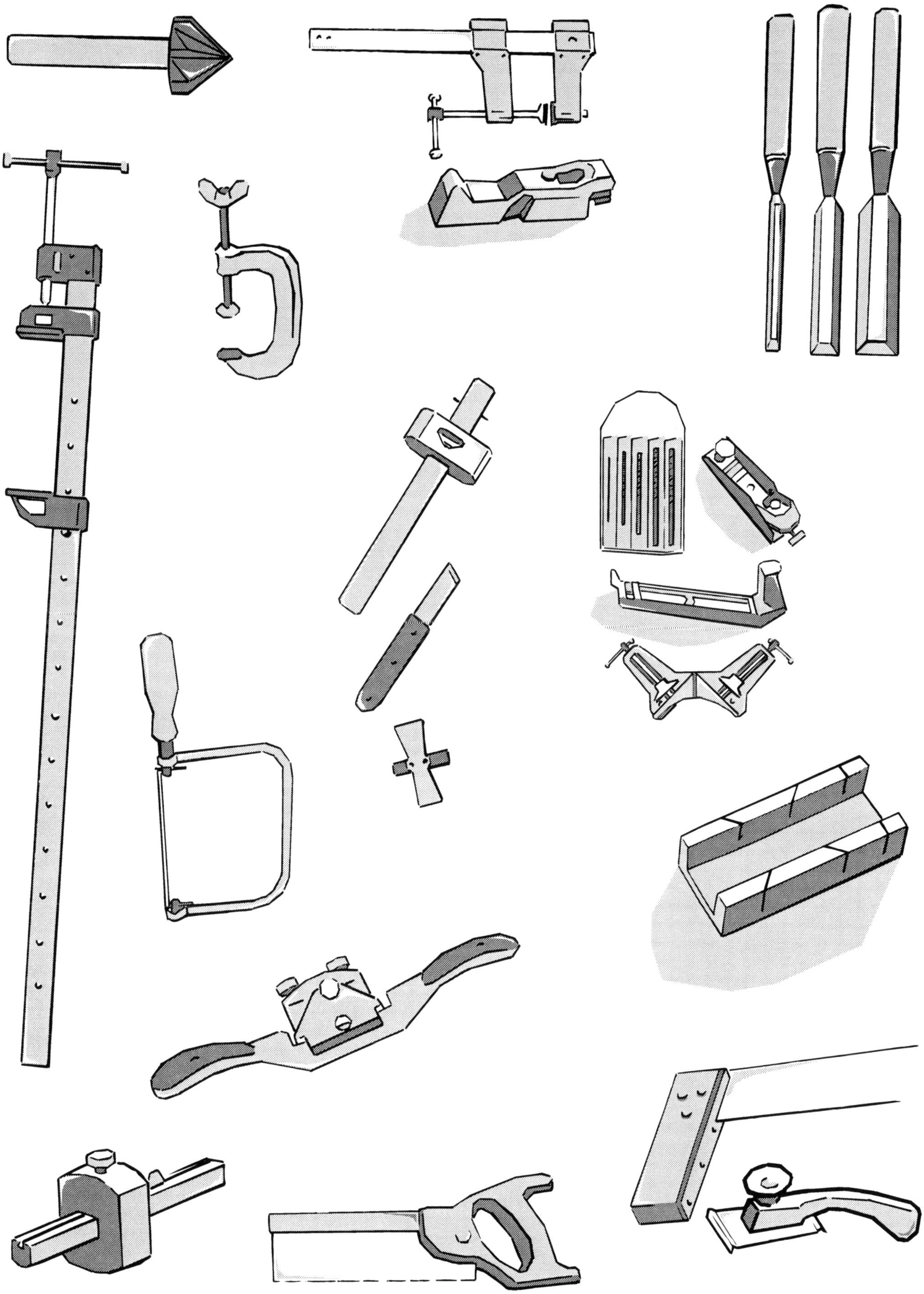

Toolbox 5 – Building and plastering

1. The history of steam power

For thousands of years humans relied on their own or their animals' muscle power for work. The Romans used the power of wind and water, but the first real source of modern power was steam.

The earliest steam engines were designed to pump water out of mines. In 1698, an English engineer called Thomas Savery built a contraption known as Miner's Friend, which used steam to drive air out of a tube. The steam was then collected by a cold water spray, causing it to condense and leaving a vacuum. Water from the mineshaft was then forced into this vacuum by outside air pressure.

In 1705, a blacksmith, Thomas Newcomen, improved this device by adding a piston in a cylinder. The piston was pushed up by the steam and then sucked down again as the steam condensed and the pressure in the cylinder fell. Both engines were inefficient because water had to be heated to steam and then cooled again.

In 1769, Scotsman James Watt separated the boiler from the cylinder so that the steam could be made continuously. He then linked his machine to a wheel that could run other machines as well as pump water. This revolutionized industry and transport throughout the world.

New machines were invented that helped spinners and weavers to make cloth more quickly and cheaply. People from the country had to move into the big cities as the newly invented machinery was too big for their homes. Before they had woven their cloth on hand looms at home in their villages but now they could not compete with the huge factories any more. Towns grew up around the factories and people lived in small brick houses built in terraces. The towns were overcrowded and dirty, and the air and rivers were polluted by the factories.

As the Industrial Revolution progressed, iron was used to build ships, and in 1802 the first working steamship, the Charlotte Dundas, was launched. But it was not before the 1830s that commercial steamships were crossing the Atlantic. Now goods could be exchanged and traded much faster than before.

But the greatest change came with the invention of the steam train in 1804. It was a steam engine on wheels. Fuel burning in the firebox heated water in the boiler until it turned to steam. The steam entered the cylinder and moved the piston. A connecting rod linked the piston to a crank on the axle of the main driving wheel, making it turn. A coupling rod connected all the driving wheels together. Exhaust steam and smoke were released from the chimney.

George Stephenson's Rocket was the first successful steam locomotive. It set a speed record of 29 mph (47 km/h) in a competition held by the new Liverpool and Manchester Railway in 1829.

In England and the United States a net of railways developed very quickly. These two countries were ahead of the world at that time in the development of the railways. By the mid-19th century, the railway network had revolutionized industry and transport in both countries.

Steam locomotives dominated the word's railway system in the 19th century. They played an important role in the Industrial Revolution – when machines were first used to do much of the work previously performed by hand – by improving the ease and the speed of transport. The use of steam power thus revolutionized the whole world and transformed most Western societies from a farming to an industrial nation using new machinery and technology.

(585 words)

2. Electric cars or hybrid engines?

Many governments throughout the world have introduced tough new laws on emission levels from car exhausts. In California, for example these laws say that by the year 2003 at least 10% of each car maker's sales must be zero emission. So there seems to be a need for efficient electric cars.

Americas, European and Japanese car producers are already doing research and there are about 20 prototypes at the moment. However, the main handicap that is still unsolved is the problem of the batteries.

The 400 kilos of lead-acid batteries just contain the energy of 5.7 liters of petrol. This means that the cars have to be light, small and streamlined. Even so the range is very limited – a mere recharge between 240 kilometers can take several hours. These are great disadvantages for a car driver who is used to a bigger car and long-distance driving.

But there are more difficulties: Although these cars can run for 200 kilometers on a dollar's worth of electricity at cheap overnight rates, its expensive batteries have to be renewed every 40,000 kilometers or so. If you take battery replacement into account, the running costs of such a car become dramatic.

But now we come the real problem.. Where do we get the additional power that is needed to recharge millions of new electric cars? Building more conventional power stations, which use fossil fuels and therefore produce high Co2 emissions, takes us back where we started.

Therefore around the world car makers are experimenting with a range of new vehicles. At the moment models which carry both an internal combustion engine and an electric motor, the so-called hybrid vehicles seem to be very popular with many designers. However, the other companies are looking into the possibilities of producing vehicles which run on alternative fuels such as hydrogen, methane or rape seed.

The advantages of hybrid cars are obvious as such a car can recover energy and store it in the battery Whenever you step on the brake pedal in your car, you are removing energy from the car. The faster a car is going, the more kinetic energy it has. The brakes of a car remove this energy and dissipate it in the form of heat. A hybrid car can capture some of this energy and store it in the battery to use later. It does this by using "regenerative braking." That is, instead of just using the brakes to stop the car, the electric motor that drives the hybrid can also slow the car. In this mode the electric motor acts as a generator and charges the batteries while the car is slowing down.

Second it can sometimes shut off the engine - A hybrid car does not need to rely on the gasoline engine all the time because it has an alternate power source, the electric motor and batteries.

Third it uses advanced aerodynamics to reduce drag – When you are driving on the freeway, most of the work your engine does goes into pushing the car through the air. This drag force can be reduced in a variety of ways. Reducing disturbances around objects that stick out from the car or eliminating them altogether can also help to improve the aerodynamics.

Last, hybrid cars use low-rolling resistance tires – that are both stiffer and inflated to a higher pressure than conventional tires. The result is that they cause about half the drag of regular tires.

In the future only the company which discovers a car which is practical, affordable and runs on a non-polluting power source will be as successful as Henry Ford when he standardized the production of the Model T.

(619 words)

3. Air-conditioning and industrialization

An air conditioner is basically a refrigerator without the insulated box. You have the same components of a refrigerator and the mechanics of the freon evaporation cycle. A typical air conditioner is doing exactly the same thing in exactly the same way.

The compressor compresses cool freon gas, causing it to become hot, high-pressure freon gas. This hot gas runs through a set of coils so it can dissipate its heat, and it condenses into a liquid in the process. The freon liquid runs through an expansion value, and in the process it evaporates to become cold, low-pressure freon gas. This cold gas runs through a set of coils that allow the gas to absorb heat and cool down the air inside the building. Mixed in with the freon is a small amount of a lightweight oil. This oil lubricates the compressor.

A split-system air conditioner splits the hot side from the cold side of the system, like this: The cold side, consisting of the expansion valve and the cold coil, is generally placed into a furnace or some other air handler. The air handler blows air through the coil and routes the air throughout the building. The hot side, known as the condensing unit, lives outside the building. In most home installations the unit looks something like this: It consists on a long spiral coil shaped like a cylinder. Inside the coil is a fan to blow air through the coil along with a weather-resistant compressor and some control logic. This approach has evolved because it is low cost and also because it normally results in reduced noise inside the house (at the expense of increased noise outside the house. In warehouses, businesses, malls, large department stores, the condensing unit normally lives on the roof and can be quite massive.

Not all southerners in the United States live in air-conditioned homes, ride air-conditioned cars, or work in air-conditioned buildings. Among rural and working-class blacks, poor whites, migrant labourers, and mountaineers, air-conditioned living is not the norm. Nevertheless, in varying degrees virtually all southerners have been affected, directly or indirectly, By the technology of climate control. Air-conditioning has influenced everything from architecture to sleeping habits and has contributed to the erosion of several regional traditions, mostly notably cultural isolation, agrarianism, romanticism, poverty, neighbourliness, strong sense of place, and a relatively slow pace of life. The net result has been a dramatic decline in regional distinctiveness.

To begin with, the air-conditioner has helped to reverse an almost century-long southern tradition of net out-migration. It was more than a coincidence that in the 50s, the decade when Air-conditioning first engulfed the South, the southern states experienced more in-migration than out-migration. The availability of air-conditioning explains why increasing numbers of Americans find it comfortable to live in the semi-tropical climate around the year. At the end of the 90s the Sunbelt now is in full swing. Helped by millions of tourists, northern migrants have brought new lifestyles to the South, disrupting the region's long-standing isolation.

Air-conditioning has also played a key role in the industrialization of the modern South. In addition to bringing new factories and businesses to the region, it has helped to improve working conditions and increase productivity. Economic growth, particularly through better working conditions, has also lead to a rising standard of living.

Air-conditioning has also fostered the urbanisation of the South: by encouraging industrialization and population growth, by acceleration the development of large public institutions and by facilitating the efficient use of urban space and opening the city to vertical, high-rise development in architecture. Without air-conditioning, skyscrapers would be less prevalent, and urban population would be smaller.

In a related development, climate control has altered attitudes toward nature and technology. Air-conditioning has taken its toll on the traditional folk culture. Human interaction has decreased significantly since the advent of air-conditioning. To confirm this point: only walk down any southern street on a hot summer afternoon, listen to the sound of the compressors and look in vain for an open window or someone in the street to talk to.

(681 words)

4. Computer Viruses

Computer Viruses are mysterious and they also get your attention. Every time a new virus hits, it makes the news if it spreads quickly. On the one hand viruses show us how unknowingly vulnerable we are, but on the other hand they show how sophisticated and interconnected human beings have become. For example, the "Melissa" virus - which became a worldwide phenomenon in March of 1999 – was so powerful that it forced Microsoft and a number of other very large companies to completely turn off their email systems until the virus could be contained. The "ILOVEYOU" virus in 2000 had a similarly devastating effect. That's pretty impressive when you consider how simple the Melissa and ILOVEYOU viruses are! Computer viruses are called "viruses" because they share some of the traits of biological viruses. A computer virus passes from computer to computer like a biological virus passes from person to person, for example. At a deeper level there are similarities as well. A computer virus must piggyback on top of some other program or document in order to get executed. Once it is running, it is then able to infect other programs or documents. Obviously the analogy between computer and biological viruses stretches things a bit, but there are enough similarities that the name sticks.

The latest thing is the email virus, and the Melissa virus in March of 1999 was spectacular. Melissa worked like this. Someone created the virus as a Word document uploaded to an Internet newsgroup. Anyone who downloaded the document and opened it would trigger the virus. The virus would then send the document (and therefore itself) in an email message to the first 50 people in the person's address book. The email message contained a friendly note that included the person's name, so the recipient would open the document thinking it was harmless. The virus would then create 50 new messages from the recipient´s machine. As a result, the Melissa virus was the fastest-spreading virus ever seen! As mentioned earlier, it forced a number of large companies to shut down their email systems.

The ILOVEYOU virus, which appeared on May 4, 2000, was even simpler. It contained a piece of code as an attachment. People who double clicked on the attachment allowed the code to execute. The code sent copies of itself to everyone in the victim's address book and then started corrupting files on the victim´s machine. The Melissa virus took advantage of the programming language built into Microsoft Word called Visual Basic for Applications. It is a complete programming language and it can be programmed to do things like modify files and send email messages. It also has a useful but dangerous auto-execute feature. A programmer can insert a program into a document that runs instantly whenever the docu-ment is opened. This is how the Melissa virus was programmed. Anyone who opened a document infected with Melissa would immediately activate the virus. It would send the 50 emails, and then infect a central file called NORMAL.DOT so that any file saved later would also contain the virus! It created a huge mess.

You can protect yourself against viruses with a few simple steps: If you are truly worried about traditional (as opposed to email) viruses, you should be running a secure operating system like UNIX or Windows NT. You never hear about viruses on these operating systems because the security features keep viruses (and unwanted human visitors) away from your hard disk. If you are using an unsecured operating system, then buying virus protection software is a nice safeguard.

If you simply avoid programs from unknown sources like the Internet, and instead stick with commercial software purchased on CDs, you eliminate almost all of the risk from traditional viruses. You should NEVER run macros in a document unless you know what they do. No normal person adds macros to a document, so avoiding all macros is a great policy.

(660 words)

Englisch	Deutsch	Weitere Bedeutungen, Verweise, Bemerkungen
access	Zugang	
accident	Unfall	
acetylene	Azetylen	
achieve, to	erreichen	
adapter	Adapter	
adjust, to	einstellen	
adjustable spanner	verstellbarer Schraubenschlüssel	
admitted, to be	eingelassen werden	
aided	unterstützt	
Allen keys	Innensechskantschlüssel	
allow, to	erlauben, lassen	
alloy	Legierung	
alumina	Tonerde	
appliances	Geräte	
appropriate	passend	
apron	Schürze	
arc	Lichtbogen	
armature	Magnetanker	
ASCII code	American Standard Code for Information and Interchange	
available, to be	erhältlich sein	
axis	die Achse	
B		
ball-pien hammer	Polierhammer	
barrier	Barriere	
basket	Korb	
batch file	Stapeldatei	
bath tub	Badewanne	
bath wrench	Badewannenschlüssel	
bearing	Lagerung	
belt	Keilriemen	
bench grindstone	Bankschleifer (Schleifstein)	
bench sander	Bankschleifer (Sandpapier)	
bend, to	biegen	
bent	verbogen	
bit	Bohrerspitze	
BIT	Binary Digit	
bleeding of radiator	entlüften	
blend	Mischung	
block plane	Handhebel	

bolster chisel	Putzmeißel	
bolt	Bolzen	
bond	Verbindung	
bottom	Boden	
bradawl	Dübelbohrer	
brass	Messing	
brazing	Messing löten	
brickayer's trowel	Maurerspachtel	
bronze	Bronze	
broom	Besen	
brushes	Bürsten	
builder's level	Wasserwage	
builder's square	Anlegewinkel	
built-in	eingebaut	
bulb	Glühlampe	
bushing	Lagerfutter	
byte	Byte	
C		
cable channel	Kabelkanal	
cable clip	Kabelschelle	
cable drum	Kabeltrommel	
CAD	Computer Aided Design	
CAE	Computer Aided Engineering	
calculate, to	berechnen	
CAM	Computer Aided Manufacturing	
camshaft	Nockenwelle	
capacity	Kapazität	
cartridge	Patrone	
catalytic converter	Kataylsator	
cause, to	verursachen	
check, to	überprüfen	
chisel	Meißel, Stechbeitel	
chuck	Bohrfutter	
CIM	Computer Integrated Manufacturing	
circlip pliers	Sicherungsringzange	
circuit	Stromkreis	
circular saw	Kreissäge	
clamp	Klammer	
claw hammer	Zimmermannshammer	

clay	Ton	
clean, to	säubern	
clinker	Schlacke	
clogged up	verstopfen	
club hammer	Fäustel	
clue	Hinweis	
CNC	Computer Numerical Control	
coarse	rauh	
coating	Beschichtung, Ummantelung	
cockspur handle lock	Schloss für Fensteröffner	
coil	Spule	
collect, to	sammlen	
combust, to	verbrennen	
combustible	brennbar	
combustion	Verbrennung	
commutator	Kommutator	
complete, to	vervollständigen	
composed of, to be	bestehen aus	
compress, to	verdichten	
compression	Verdichtung	
compressor	Verdichter	
concrete	Beton	
concrete mixer	Betonmischer	
condenser	Kondensator	
conductor	Leiter	
connections	Verbindung	
consumer unit	Verbrauchseinheit	
consumption	Verbrauch	
contain, to	beinhalten	
coping saw	Laubsäge	
copper	Kupfer	
corner trowel	Winkelspachtel	
correct, to	verbessern	
countersink	Spitzsenker	
cracked	gesprungen	
cramp	Schraubzwinge	
crankshaft	Kurbelwelle	
create, to	erschaffen	
crush, to	zermahlen	
current	Strom	

D - E

curtain rail	Duschstange	
D		
deadlocks	Sicherheitsschloss	
deliver, to	herausgeben	
delivery	Übergabe	
demostrate, to	verdeutlichen	
dented	verbeult	
design, to	entwerfen	
device	Gerät, Vorrichtung	
directory	Verzeichnis	
discolour, to	sich verfärben	
dissolve, to	sich auflösen	
distributer	der Verteiler	
DIY	Do it yourself	
dovetail marker	Schwalbenschwanzmarker	
dovetail saw	Schwalbenschwanzsäge	
drain	Abfluss	
drill sharpener	Bohrerschleifgerät	
drill stand	Bohrständer	
drive	Laufwerk	
driven, to be	angetrieben werden	
dump	Abfall, Versteck	
E		
earth clamp	Erdungsklammer	
earth rammer	Erdstampfer	
eat, to	zerfressen (Rost)	
economic	sparsam	
elbow fitting	Ellbogengelenk, Kniestück	
electricity supply	Elekrizitätsversorgung	
electrocution	Elektroschock	
electrode holder	Elektrodenhalter	
emission	Ausstoß	
emit, to	ausstrahlen	
ensure, to	sich versichern	
escape, to	entweichen	
examine, to	untersuchen	
exhaust	Auspuff	
exhaust valve	Auslassventil	
expand, to	sich ausdehnen	

face mask	Gesichtsmaske	
fall, to	fallen	
fan	Ventilator	
feed, to	Daten eingeben, nachfüllen	
fibre optic	Glasfaser	
file	Datei	
file	Feile	
filler metal	Füllmetal	
filthy	schmutzig	
find, to	herausfinden	
fire extinguisher	Feuerlöscher	
fit, to	einpassen	
fittings	Passung	
fix, to	fixieren	
flex	bewegliches Kabel	
flexible drill shaft	Schnellspannfutter	
flush socket	Steckdose unter Putz	
flux	Flussmittel	
flywheel	Schwungrad	
forced, to be	gedrungen werden	
forerunner	Vorläufer	
fret saw	Laubsäge	
fuel chamber	Brennstoffkammer	
function, to	funktionieren	
fuse	Sicherung	
fuse, to	verschmelzen	
G		
g cramp	Schraubzwinge	
gang	Reihenschaltung	
gap	Spalte	
gas blowlamp	Lötlampe	
gas cylinder	Gasflasche	
gas flow	Gasfluss	
gasket	Dichtung	
gate valve	Absperrhahn	
goggles	Schutzbrille	
gravel	Kieselsteine	
grease	Schmiermittel	
grind, to	zermahlen	
grinding points	Schleifköpfe, Schleifspitzen	

G - H - I - J

grindstone	Schleifstein	
gypsum	Gips	
H		
hacksaw	Eisensäge	
hand bender	Handbiegegerät	
handwheel valve	Eckventil	
hardware	Gerät	
hawk	Mörtelbrett	
hold, to	halten	
hole saw	Lochsäge	
hook scraper	Hakenkratzer	
hose	Schlauch	
hydrogen	Wasserstoff	
I		
IEE	Institute of Electrical Engineers	
ignite, to	zünden	
ignition	die Zündung	
influence, to	beeinflussen	
inject, to	einspritzen	
inlet valve	Einlassventil	
input	Eingabe	
installed, to be	installiert sein	
insulate, to	isolieren	
insulated	isoliert	
intake	Einlass	
integrated	integriert	
interface	Schnittstelle	
invent, to	erfinden	
involve, to	beinhalten	
iron core	Eisenkern	
isolate, to	isolieren	
J		
jaws	Bohrfutterbacken	
jet	Düse, Strahlrohr	
jigsaw	Stechsäge	
join, to	verbinden	
joint	Verbindung	
jointing paste	Dichtpaste	
joy-stick	Schaltknüppel	
junior hacksaw	kleine Eisensäge	

keyboard	Tastatur	
kill, to	kaputt machen	
kiln	Brennofen	
L		
LAN	Local Area Network	
lead	Blei	
LED	Light Emitting Diode	
lever	Hebel	
lime	Kalk	
limestone	Kalkstein	
line and pins	Richtschnur	
liquid solder	flüssiges Lot	
live	unter Strom	
M		
magnetic field	das Magnetfeld	
mains	Hauptkabel	
mains tester	Spannungsprüfer	
maintenance	Wartung	
manifold	Einlasskrümmer	
MAP	Manufacturing Automation Protocol	
marking gauge	Passlehre	
marking knife	Markiermesser	
mat	Matte	
matching, to be	passend sein	
medicine chest	Medizinschränkchen	
melt, to	schmelzen	
memory	Speicher	
message	Nachricht	
meter	Ablesegerät, Zähler	
minute	winzig	
mitre box	Gehrlade	
mitre cramp	Gehrungskrampe	
mixing shovel	Schaufel	
modem	Modem	
modify, to	verändern	
mole wrench	Gripzange	
monitor	Bildschirm	
mortise gauge	Zapfenstreichmaß	
mounted	befestigt	

M - N - O - P

muddy	verdreckt, schlammig	
multiply, to	vermehren	
N		
nail punches	Körner	
neat	sauber, ordentlich	
need, to	benötigen	
nip,to	klemmen	
nippers	Kneifzange	
nozzle	Düse	
nut	Mutter	
nut and bolt	Mutter und Bolzen	
O		
obstructed	versperrt	
OCR	Operical Character Recognition	
open spanner	Maulschlüssel	
operate, to	bedienen	
opposite	gegensätzlich	
outlet	Auslass	
output	Ausgabe	
overheat, to	überhitzen	
oxygen	Sauerstoff	
P		
pad	Unterlage	
peeled	abgeblättert	
permanent magnet	Dauermagnet	
PFTE tape	Isolierband	
pillar tap	Standarmatur	
pin hammer	Zapfenhammer	
pipe clip	Rohrschelle	
pipe cutter	Rohrschneider	
pipe wrench	Rohrzange	
piston	Kolben	
piston rod	die Kolbenstange	
pit	Grube	
pit, to	sich festfressen (Kolben)	
plaster	Putz	
plasterer's trowl	Putzkelle	
pliers	Zange	
plotter	Zeichengerät	
plug	Stecker	

plugging chisel	Stechbeitel	
poisonous	giftig	
pole	Pol	
pollutant	Schadstoff	
pot	Tiegel, Gefäß	
pour out, to	ausgießen	
powerful	kräftig	
pressure	Druck	
pressure gauge	Druckanzeige	
pressure regulator	Druckregulator	
prevent, to	vermeiden	
printer	Drucker	
process, to	verarbeiten	
processor	Prozessor	
produce, to	herstellen	
propel, to	antreiben	
protocol	Fertigung	
prototype	Richtmodell	
provide, to	zur Verfügung stellen, beschaffen	
pushed, to be	gedrückt werden	
put around, to	herumlegen	
R		
RAM	Random Access Memory	
rebate plane	Holzhobel	
recognition	Erkennung	
recorder	Aufnahmegerät	
reinforce, to	verstärken	
release, to	lösen	
remove, to	entfernen	
repel, to	abstoßen	
require, to	benötigen	
research	Forschung	
reset, to	zurückstellen	
resistance	Widerstand	
retrieval	Wiederfinden	
retrieval system	Verarbeitungssystem	
retrieve, to	zurückholen	
rim latch	Schnappschloss	
ring spanner	Ringschlüssel	
rive pliers	Nietzange	

R - S

ROM	Read Only Memory	
rotate, to	sich drehen	
rusty	verrostet	
S		
sander	Sandpapierschleifer	
sash cramp	verstellbare Schraubzwinge	
sawblades	Sägeblätter	
scales	Waage	
scan, to	einlesen	
scanner	Lesegerät	
scratched	verkratzt	
scratcher	Schaber	
select, to	auswählen	
sense, to	aufspüren	
service	Wartung	
sheathing	Kabelisolierung	
shovel	Schaufel	
shower head	Duschkopf	
silicia	Kieselerde	
simulate, to	simulieren	
sink	Spülbecken	
sink mixer	Mischbatterie	
slam, to	zuwerfen (Tür)	
slit	Schlitz, Spalt	
socket spanner	Stackdose	
solder	Lötzinn, Weichlot	
soldering	Löten	
solve, to	lösen	
spade	Spaten	
spark	Funke	
spark plug	Zündkerze	
spin around, to	herumdrehen	
spokeshave	Schabeisen	
spot	Stelle, Punkt	
stained	befleckt	
standard hacksaw	Eisensäge	
stem	Stamm, Ventilschaft	
stiff broom	Besen	
stop valve	Absperrventil	
storage	Speicherung	

store, to	speichern	
stored, to be	gelagert werden	
streamer	Datensicherungsgerät	
strengthen, to	verstärken	
strip connector	Lüsterklemmen	
stroke	Takt	
suck, to	einsaugen	
supplied, to be	versorgt sein	
surface socket	Steckdose auf Putz	
surform files	(Spezialfeile)	
T		
tank cutter	Lochschneider	
tap	Wasserhahn	
tarnished	angelaufen, fleckig	
tee fitting	Rohrverbindungsstück	
terminal block	Anschlussklemme	
thermostatic valve	Thermostat	
thickness	Dicke	
tiles	Fliesen	
timber	Bauholz	
tin	Zinn, Blech	
tinsnips	Blechschere	
tiny	winzig	
tip	Spitze	
top	Oberteil, Spitze	
torch	Taschenlampe	
torpedo switch	Kabelschalter	
towel rack	Handtuchablage	
track lifter	Fugenzieher	
translate, to	übertragen	
transmit, to	übermitteln	
trap	Siphon, Geruchsverschluss	
travel, to	strömen	
trowel	Kelle	
try sqaure	Richtscheit	
tube	Röhre	
twist drill	Spiralbohrer	
twisted	verbogen	
U		
undo, to	lösen	

U - V - W

use, to	benutzen	
utilise, to	verwenden	
V		
valve	Ventil	
vaporise, to	verflüchtigen	
volatile	flüchtig	
W		
washer	Dichtungsring, Unterlegscheibe	
weld, to	schweißen	
welding gloves	Schweißhandschuhe	
welding rod	Schweißstab	
welding torch	Schweißbrenner	
well-insulated	gut isoliert	
wheelbarrow	Schubkarre	
wing nut	Flügelmutter	
wire	Draht	
wire wool	Drahtwolle	
wodden float	Holzkelle	
workpiece	Werkstück	
worn	verbraucht	
wrecking bar	Brechstange	